WEDDING HUMOUR

(WHO BETTER TO RECALL WEDDING JOKES AND STORIES THAN CLERGYMEN. SO WE WROTE TO CLERGYMEN ALL OVER N.IRELAND AND BEYOND).

COMPILED BY

JILLIAN BOYD
SHONA KIRK
ELIZABETH SIMMONS
7th COLERAINE GIRL GUIDE COMPANY

ILLUSTRATED BY

GRAHAM PATTERSON

FOREWORD

by

Rev.Thomas Magowan

Minister Coleraine Methodist Church

I heartily congratulate the initiative shown by the girls of the Guide Company to aid our Church Restoration Fund. It is a book I feel that will be much sought after by aspiring speech makers at weddings.

Those of us in the ranks of the clergy, who are called upon to conduct and participate in many marriage services, find ourselves constantly searching for fresh material to add to our repertoire of stories. Here is just the thing we need.

The response of those asked to provide material was tremendous. I wish to express my personal thanks to all the contributors. Without their help there would be no book. Some of you sent a donation as well, which was a great encouragement to the girls.

I hope that you will find much to chuckle over as you read these pages. Please commend it to others and so help a worthy cause.

Thomas Magowan

REV.CANON W.J.R.BENSON

16 Ratheane Avenue
COLERAINE

At a Wedding Anniversary dinner to celebrate 37 years of married life the man replying to the toast told his audience that he and his wife had made a "BARGAIN" right at the beginning.

It was that she could make all the small decisions, but if a big problem arose she would agree that he should make the decision.

Just imagine he said how fortunate we have been in all our married life, - that even after 37 years we have never had to make a big decision yet!

Rev Denis Bambrick

38 Knockhill Park
Belfast

Mary to her fiance, John, "Wouldn't it be lovely if we could bring my mother on our honeymoon trip to Kenya on Safari."

John, "Yes dear, that would be just lovely!" During the night on Safari they heard an ENORMOUS ROAR and looking out they saw twenty paces away from mother, who because of the heat had taken a walk from her little tent,

A LION, TAIL TWITCHING ETC. - READY TO 'POUNCE'.

Mary, "Oh John darling - YOU MUST DO SOMETHING".

John, "its all right dear, the lion has got himself into this fix, let him get himself out of it".

REV. W. H. PEDEN

54 Sydenham Avenue
BELFAST
BT4 2DS

A young soldier had just become engaged to be married when he was told he was to be posted overseas for three years.
He promised his fiancee that he would write a letter each day and he remained faithful to his promise. But before his three years tour of duty had ended his fiancee married the post man.

A husband and wife were in bed when a heavy lorry crashed into their house, smashing the front wall. The bed slid out into the garden from the collapsed floor. When the initial shock passed, the wife said to her husband, "Do you realize it Tom, this is the first time we have been out of the house together for five years!"

Two men were discussing the possibility of Flying Saucers after a short discussion
Bill said "Oh yes I believe in Flying Saucers, but I didn't think about'em nor experience it until after I got married!"

A young couple got married and after the reception party was over, they went to bed. They weren't in bed very long until the young lady complained of feeling cold. The husband got up immediately, went downstairs and filled a hot water bottle, and told his wife that she would soon be warmed up. A little later she complained again, so out her husband got, went downstairs, and brought up some of the blankets they had received as wedding presents. He put these on to the bed and told his wife, that with the blankets and the hot water bottle she would soon be all right.

Very soon she was complaining of the cold once more, and she said to him, "You know, before we got married I used to sleep in the same bed as my sister, and whenever we felt cold we used to give each other a big hug."

To this her husband said, "Well dear, I'm very sorry, but there's no way I'm going to get the car out, drive 50 miles to get your sister here tonight!"

Stormont Presbyterian Church

618 Upper Newtownards Road, Belfast BT4 3HA Phone 656637

Minister
Rev. Dr. J. Ronald Savage
1 Knockdarragh Park
Belmont Road
Belfast BT4 2LE
Phone 763155

Clerk of Session
Dr. John Patton
7 Knockdarragh Park
Belmont Road
Belfast BT4 2LE
Phone 63401

Secretary
Mr. Jim Irvine
25 Kensington Road
Knock
Belfast BT5 6NH
Phone 794279

Treasurer
Mr. Colin Boyd
43 Knocklofty Park
Belfast BT4 3NB
Phone 671605

The best man was reading apologies from the people absent.

He read one from a friend of the bride's father "Joe Murphy is sorry he is not able to come because he's one hundred and eleven today."

The groom gave him a nudge and whispered something,

"Sorry that should have read, Joe Murphy is sorry he is not able to come along because he's <u>ill</u> today!"

Lambeth Palace London SE1 7JU

3rd May 1990

From the Archbishop's Chaplain

Dear Elizabeth,

The Archbishop has asked me to thank you for your letter and to reply on his behalf.

The following story is his contribution to your book on Wedding Humour:

I once told a nervous couple at their marriage that they need not worry. 'I will whisper to you exactly what you are to do. Just obey me.'

The custom at a wedding service is usually to take the first part at the chancel step, and then, for the prayers, the priest and the bridal couple process to the altar. After I had finished the first part a hymn struck up. I whispered to the kneeling couple, 'Follow me'. I turned round to lead them to the altar. On arrival I turned to them again (it was quite a distance in this church) and to my amazement found them crawling after me on their hands and knees. I had not said, 'Stand up and follow me'.

This comes with good wishes for the success of the book, and the hope that it raises a lot of money for your church restoration fund.

Yours sincerely,

Graham James

The Revd. Canon Graham James

Miss E. Simmons
3 Apollo Crescent
Portrush
BT56 8SA

REV CANON R M WILKINSON

60 Coleraine Road
PORTRUSH

They were celebrating their first wedding anniversary and she told her husband that she had visited the doctor during the day.

"Why?" he asked "Have you Asian flu?"
"No" came the reply. "I've Egyptian flu."
"What does that mean?"

"I'm going to be a mummy!"

The shy young bride was really upset when she learned that her handsome, middle-aged husband had been married twice previously.
Through her tears, she asked what had become of her two predecessors.
"Well I may as well tell you," said her spouse.
"My first wife died of mushroom poisoning."
"And your second wife?" she insisted.
"She died of a fractured skull," he replied.
"It was her own fault - she wouldn't eat the mushrooms."

SECOND KILREA PRESBYTERIAN CHURCH
Co. Londonderry

MINISTER:
REV. RICHARD N. GORDON, B.Sc. B.D. Ph.D
Drumane Manse, 40 Blackrock Road,
Kilrea, Coleraine, BT51 5XH
Phone: KILREA 40258

SECRETARY:
MR. T. K. WOODS,
Woodlands, 23 Moneygran Road,
Kilrea, Coleraine, BT51 5SJ
Phone: KILREA 40208

CLERK OF SESSIONS:
MR. G. A. McILRATH, O.B.E., J.P.
The Lorne, 20 Fallahogey Road,
Kilrea, Coleraine, BT51 5ST
Phone: KILREA 40269

TREASURER:
MR. JOHN E. McILRATH,
The Lorne, 20 Fallahogey Road,
Kilrea, Coleraine, BT51 5ST
Phone: KILREA 40269

Three honeymoon couples were breakfasting together in a lovely hotel.
The first husband from Kilrea said to his bride,
"Pass the honey, Sugar."
The second husband, from Garvagh, said to his bride,
"Pass the sugar, Sweetie."
The hard husband, from Coleraine, after much prompting by his bride could only manage,
"Pass the tea, Bag!!!"

A minister planning a wedding service, with a couple whose romance up to that point had been, to date stormy asked them what hymns they wished to sing. They replied, simultaneously, "Fight the good fight, with all thy might."

SECOND KILREA PRESBYTERIAN CHURCH
Co. Londonderry

MINISTER:
REV. RICHARD N. GORDON, B.Sc. B.D. Ph.D
Drumane Manse, 40 Blackrock Road,
Kilrea, Coleraine, BT51 5XH
Phone: KILREA 40258

SECRETARY:
MR. T. K. WOODS,
Woodlands, 23 Moneygran Road,
Kilrea, Coleraine, BT51 5SJ
Phone: KILREA 40208

CLERK OF SESSIONS:
MR. G. A. McILRATH, O.B.E., J.P.
The Lorne, 20 Fallahogey Road.
Kilrea, Coleraine, BT51 5ST
Phone: KILREA 40269

TREASURER:
MR. JOHN E. McILRATH,
The Lorne, 20 Fallahogey Road.
Kilrea, Coleraine, BT51 5ST
Phone: KILREA 40269

Have you heard of the man from Upper Tamlaght who came to Coleraine to buy a ticket to travel to China.

"Please can I have a ticket for China?"

They sold him a ticket to Belfast.
In Belfast he repeated his request and was sold a ticket to Larne, and in easy stages was sold tickets from Stranraer to London, London to Dover, Dover to Calais, etc, etc...

After a glorious month in China he decided to come home and went to a travel agent and asked him for a ticket to Tamlaght.

The immediate reply was "Is that Upper or lower Tamlaght?"

Dublin
Central
Mission
of the
Methodist Church
in Ireland

THE ALTADORE PROJECT

Social Aid Centre, Marlborough Place, Dublin 1.
Tel.: 742123/744668

Ministers:
Rev. Desmond C. Bain, Superintendent.
Rev. David Kilpatrick

Hon Treasurers: David Lee & T.W. Rowlett Morris, F.C.A.,
Development Director: Arthur Nowlan, A.C.I.S., D.P.A.

"In the Church of Ireland Marriage Service, there used to be a promise taken by the groom, which included these words ... with all my worldly goods I thee endow. One, not so young newly wed husband, discovered a little of what this could mean. At the reception after the wedding ceremony he always seemed to be the last to finish each course. In fact, he allowed the food to sit in front of him until it was almost cold, whilst his bride tucked in with much delight.

By the time the dessert came round the waiter was a bit concerned and asked him if everything was alright. The groom nodded and the waiter then enquired, "But why are you not eating sir?"

The Groom responded with a pronounced lisp, "I'm waiting for Agnesh to finish with the teeth!"

Rev.K.G.PATTERSON

27 Moneyleck Rd
RASHARKIN

This couple were going on their honeymoon out in the Wild West of America. They were travelling by horse and cart. Things were going along nicely when all of a sudden the horse stopped. The man got down from the cart to see what had happened. Apparently nothing was wrong, so he spoke sharply to the horse and said,
"Right now this is your first warning."
He got back on the cart and the horse went a little bit further, then again for no reason it stopped. The man again got off the cart, spoke sharply to the horse and said,
"Now that's your second warning."
On they went a little further and as they were climbing this little hill the horse again stopped and refused to move. The man got off the cart shouted at the horse and then took his gun and shot the horse through the head. At this point his bride began to remonstrate with her husband and told him there was no sense in his action, calling him all kinds of names. He replied to her "I'll do what I like - THIS IS YOUR FIRST WARNING!"

IRELAND
DIVISION

THE SALVATION ARMY

4 CURTIS STREET • BELFAST • BT1 2ND • NORTHERN IRELAND
Telephone Belfast 324730

27th June, 1990

Elizabeth Simmons
7th Coleraine Guides
Methodist Church Hall,
Queen Street,
COLERIANE.

Dear Elizabeth,

I am writing to you on behalf of Major William Main as he has asked me to inform you of a humourous wedding situation. As a wedding ceremony is a very serious and solemn occasion the Major informs me that nothing humourous has happened in any wedding services that he has conducted. However, I did once hear of a situation when somebody was asked to read the Bible at a wedding. They were asked to read 1 John 4:7 which reads: 'Love is made complete among us so that we will have confidence on the day of judgement, because in this world we are like Him. There is no fear in love. But perfect love drives out fear, because fear has to do with punishment. The man who fears is not made perfect in love. We love because He first loved us.' v. 17-19 N.I.V.

Instead of reading this lovely passage of Scripture, the person stood up and read from John 4: 17 which says: "I have no husband," she replied. Jesus said to her, "You are right when you say that you have no husband. The fact is, you have had five husbands, and the man you now have is not your husband. What you have just said is quite true."

I am sure that you can see the difference and can imagine how the bride and groom must have felt! I trust that this will be' of some use to you.

God bless you.

Yours sincerely,

Gladys Thompson

Gladys Thompson
Captain
Divisional Assistant

PORTSTEWART

An absent-minded Minister had a problem keeping to his subject. A friend suggested it would help if the Minister had an amusing anecdote which could be used to introduce the theme.

"For example", said the friend, at a wedding you could use the jingle

"THE HAPPIEST MOMENTS OF MY LIFE
WERE SPENT IN THE ARMS OF ANOTHER MAN'S WIFE."

Then pause ... and say, "MY MOTHER!"

The Minister decided that this was a good aid to memory and at the very next wedding reception he began his speech with the lines

"THE HAPPIEST MOMENTS OF MY LIFE
WERE SPENT IN THE ARMS OF ANOTHER MAN'S WIFE."

He then paused to allow for the dramatic conclusion but instead he said, "AND I CAN'T FOR THE LIFE OF ME REMEMBER WHO IT WAS!"

From F. L. S.

BALLYCASTLE PRESBYTERIAN CHURCH

CASTLE STREET BALLYCASTLE BT54 6AS

Minister:
VERY REV. A. W. G. BROWN,
B.A., Ph.D., D.D.
The Manse, 28 Quay Road,
Ballycastle, BT54 6BH
Tel.: (02657) 62231

Clerk of Session:
D. H. McCONAGHIE
35 Whitepark Road,
Ballycastle. BT54 6LL
Tel.: (02657) 62442

Church Secretary:
R. D. McCONAGHIE,
36 Ann Street,
Ballycastle, BT54 6AD
Tel.: (02657) 62400

Treasurer:
N. MAWHINNEY
27 Strandview Road,
Ballycastle. BT54 6AJ
Tel.: (02657) 62172

20th February, 1990.

Dear Jillian,

Very many thanks for your letter. It was good to hear from you and to learn about your plans to produce a book of Wedding Humour in aid of your Church Restoration Fund. I do hope your plans will work out well, and that when the book comes out I shall be able to buy a copy of it. Sorry it took me so long to reply, but life is really busy at present.

Well, here is my wedding story:

When the young couple came back form their honeymoon, they were very much in love. Every evening when he came home from work, and rang the doorbell, she ran eagerly to the door to let him in. 'Is that my wee hubzy-wubzy home for his dinzy-winzy?' she would say. And then the door would be flung open and they would fall into each other's arms in a long and tender embrace. One evening she heard the doorbell a few moments earlier than usual.. She whipped of her apron, and fluffed up her hair, and ran eagerly to the door. As usual she spoke out through the letter-box, 'Is that my wee hubzy-wubzy home for his dinzy-winzy?' A gruff voice at the other side of the door replied, 'No Ma'am. It's the plumbzy-wumzy here to mend the sinky-winky.'

I hope you haven't got that one already! Well many thanks again for asking me, and all the best with your book.

Yours sincerely,

A W Godfrey Brown

REV DAVID ALDERDICE

21 Old Galgorm Rd
BALLYMENA

Lady was cleaning upstairs window on the Newtownards Road in Belfast. She slipped and fell through it into a dustbin on the footpath below.

A coloured man passing by was heard to say "White man very extravagant throwing away a good woman like that!!"

A man was weeping at a grave and saying over and over,
"Why did you die?" A passerby heard him and offered sympathy,
"Is that your wife's grave?"
"No, No, - it was my wife's first husband!"

REV. T.S. LINDSAY
The Manse,
37 Station Road,
Garvagh,
Co. Londonderry
BT51 5LA
Tel: 58220

A young courting couple were out walking one night. The young man turned to the young lady and said

"WILL YOU MARRY ME?"

"Of course I will", replied the young lady as quick as lightning.

They walked on! There was a silence for a goodly while.

"Why are you so quiet asked the young lady?"

"Oh!" said the young man,"I think I have maybe said too much already."

A minister told his congregation there were no perfect people. RIGHTLY SO!

"If anyone thinks he is perfect - let him stand up" said the minister.

A man got up on his feet at the back.

"Sir - are you claiming to be perfect", inquired the minister!

"No!" replied the Man - "I'm standing proxy for my wife's first husband."

REV.J.E.KENNEDY

38, Prospect Road
PORTSTEWART

Mary and John had been going out together for over 20 years. As Mary thought John was a bit slow about proposing marriage she said to him one evening -

"John did you know the people around us are beginning to talk about us."

"And what are these gossips saying about us?" said John.

"They are saying we are going to get married" said Mary.

"Well", says John "And sure who would marry either of us at our age?"

REV H HOPKINS

THE RECTORY
10 COLERAINE RD
PORTRUSH

First man: "How did you get on with Miss Smart after the dance last night?"

Second man: "Well, I asked her twice if I could see her home, and she said that as I was so keen on seeing her home she would send me a photograph of it."

CHURCH OF IRELAND

Seapatrick Parish

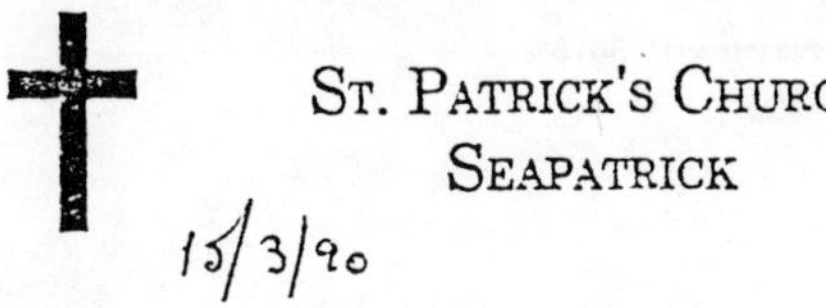

HOLY TRINITY CHURCH
BANBRIDGE

ST. PATRICK'S CHURCH
SEAPATRICK

15/3/90

REV JOHN SCOTT

ADVICE TO NEW BRIDE

TREAT YOUR HUSBAND LIKE A DOG

Keep him well Groomed

Keep him well Fed

Give him plenty of Exercise

and Never let him out at night.

Burnside Presbyterian Church

Senior Minister:
The Rev. E. M. Borland, B.A.

PORTSTEWART

6 Whyns Crescent,
Portstewart.
Co. Londonderry.
BT55 7HS

☎ Portstewart 3016

5/2/90

A French lady who spoke very little English once came to London, hailed a taxicab and asked the taxi-driver how much he would charge to take her to her hotel. A figure was agreed, but the traffic in London was heavy and the taxi had to take to side-streets to reach their destination. When the lady offered the agreed sum, the taxi-driver pointed to the meter on his cab and explained that he had to make detours to get there and so the charge was greater than what had been agreed. Reluctantly the French lady paid up but remarked,

"Vous am dearer to me now zan when we engaged!"

I'm sure the bride to-day is dearer to the bridegroom "zan when they engaged".

The Bishop of Down and Dromore

The Rt. Rev. Dr. Gordon McMullan

The See House, 32 Knockdene Park South,
Belfast BT5 7AB

AN AMERICAN WEDDING STORY

At a wedding reception the best man explained that it was his task to say something about the groom. As they had been class-mates at the University of Maryland, the best man thought it would be interesting to use each initial of their University to highlight a particular quality of the groom. Beginning with 'M' for methodical, he slowly picked his way through all the other letters in "Maryland".

This was a rather boring exercise for some of the guests and went on for a long time. Before the best-man had reached the end of his speech one guest whispered to another that he feared the best-man would never finish. The reply came back from the other guest - "Oh well thank goodness they weren't fellow students at the Massachusetts Institute of Technology!"

Bill Nesbitt

THE WEDDING SERVICE

A certain country clergyman was married to a wife
Who moaned and nagged and tortured him, and terrorised his life -
He'd had enough ... and when, one day, a couple came to wed.
He glowered on the bridegroom, and this is what he said ...

'Now, will you take this woman to lawfully be wedded,
To tongue and persecute you in a way you've always dreaded?
To order all your movements, like a puppet on a string,
To take away your freedom now you've flung your final fling?

'Will you promise to obey her when she issues a command,
And tell the fellows in the pub that, sadly, you've been banned?
And guarantee that you'll fulfil her wildest dreams and wishes,
And help with all the housework, and wash and dry the dishes?

'Will you vacuum all the carpets, and polish all the floors,
And clean the dirty windows, and do the other chores?
When there's something you've decided that you'll watch on television
Will you swear that you won't grumble when she alters your decision?

'Will you pledge that you won't argue, and never, ever fight,
And realise the bitter truth that she is always right?
Will you always love and cherish her, and show her that you care -
Even when the sight of her is more than you can bear?

'Will you settle all the household bills (believe me, they'll be many!),
And pander to her fancies 'till you're left with not a penny?
Are you prepared to always strive to do the best you can -
And finish up the way I have, a badly broken man?

Bill Nesbitt

THE WEDDING SERVICE (Cont'd.)

'Will you assure me, here and now, that you will not complain
Every time she tells you she's a headache (once again) -
And if some pretty miss comes by, will you avert your eyes,
And think sweet thoughts ... and never envy all the single guys?

'Will you accept the fact that you will be her lifelong slave,
Your only hope of freedom is a peaceful, early grave?
Are you prepared to face a life that's going to be rough -
Knowing that your very best is never good enough?

'If that's the sort of life you want, then, son, it's up to you,
So, if you dare, then speak up now, and answer me "I do" ...' -
But when the clergyman looked up, I'm very sad to say,
The blushing bride stood all alone - the groom had run away ...!

Rev. & Mrs. S. A. Finlay
The Manse
156 Glassdrumman Road
Annalong
NEWRY BT34 4QL

A Farmer married a rather well-to-do lady. Some time later he was showing some friends round his farm and telling them about some recent acquisitions. His wife followed the group round.

First he showed them his new milking parlour. All were impressed, but his wife muttered in the background ... "If it wasn't for my money it wouldn't be there." Again he showed them a new tractor. All were impressed, but the muttering in the background was heard again ... "If it wasn't for my money it wouldn't be there."

Finally he showed the group a new silo. A third time his wife's muttering voice was heard ... "If it wasn't for my money it wouldn't be there." At this the farmer could take no more. He turned to his wife and said ... "If it wasn't for your money <u>you</u> wouldn't be here!"

Rev J. B. Mooney

BELFAST

Second Wife

Man: "Doctor, could you come round quickly, I think my wife has appendicitis."

Doctor: "She couldn't have appendicitis because I had her appendix removed five or six years ago. Have you ever heard of anyone having a second appendix?"

Man: Doctor, have you never heard of a man having a second wife?"

REV CANON WILKINSON

60 Coleraine Road
PORTRUSH

"Darling" said Mrs Newlywed, "how will we manage for money when we start a family?"

"Don't worry, my pet," replied the groom, "I'll go out and get you a better job."

After six months of marriage, they were having their first argument. He lost his temper completely, and struck his wife across the face.

The Vicar, who happened to be passing the window, saw it happen and rushed into the house.

The man, on seeing the Vicar coming in, quickly regained his composure. He gave his wife another smack across the face and shouted,
"Now will you go to church!"

NEW ROW PRESBYTERIAN CHURCH
COLERAINE

Minister: Rev. D. H. ALLEN, M.A., B.D.
THE MANSE, 24 GRANGE ROAD,
COLERAINE, N. IRELAND
Telephone: Coleraine42032
(026542032)

23/9/90

Rev.D.H.Allen,M.A.,B.D.

WEDDING STORIES

Tommy was just mad about tractors, he had model and working tractors all over his room. The walls were covered with pictures and posters of tractors and he had three or four different models in the back yard.

He met and fell in love with a very pretty girl, but she just could not stand his craze for tractors. She felt second best in his life, so when he popped the question, she agreed on condition that he would get rid of all the tractors ... big ones, little one, pictures, posters, the lot.

To everyones amazement Tommy agreed, they got married. One day he was in a shop when a fire broke out and began to spread quickly. Tommy pushed the people to the side, sucked in his breath deeply and as the fire went out, the shopkeeper came up and thanked him.

"How did you do that?" he asked.

"Oh, it was no trouble at all," replied Tommy, "You see I'm an EX-TRACTOR FAN!"

REV G. R. MINCHIN

4 Fortview PORTBALLINTRAE BUSHMILLS

Some years after they were married a young couple were revisting the scenes of their courtship days.

As they strolled along they were inclined to be a bit sentimental. When they came to a certain corner, she became very sentimental.

"Darling dear do you remember the times we used to meet here?"

"I do that," he replied, "but that sign wasn't there then."

Looking at the sign she read,

DANGEROUS CORNER, GO SLOW.

TRUE STORY

A very shy, bashful, young man went to interview his minister about getting married. On arrival at the ministers house, after dark, he was shown to the study. He put his head around the door and the following conversation took place.

John, "Can you do it Sir?"

Minister, "Yes, John, When?"

John, "Tomorrow morning."

Minister, "What time?"

John, "Eleven o'clock, Good night Sir."

First Dunboe Presbyterian Church

Minister:
REV. J.A. McCAUGHAN, B.Sc., B.D.
1st Dunboe Manse, 111 Mussenden Road, Castlerock BT51 4TU
Tel: Castlerock 848276

20th January 1990

Dear Jillian,

Thank you very much for the opportunity to contribute to your book of "Wedding Humour". I hope that it is a great success and raises thousands for your Restoration Fund ! I look forward to buying a copy myself. I like to tell the following joke at weddings :-

A bride was very nervous at the wedding rehearsal and found it very difficult to remember where she had to go, and what she had to do. Eventually the minister decided to make it as simple as possible for her. "First" he said,"You come up the aisle. Then you move forward to the altar. And finally we sing a hymn." The bride seemed much happier with this explanation, and the minister thought there would be no problem. Imagine his surprise, and the astonishment of the entire congregation at the wedding: as she entered the church she could be heard saying to herself over and over again, "Aisle - altar - hymn. Aisle - altar - hymn." Everyone thought she was saying "I'll alter him."!

I hope that you have lots of fun with your excellent idea.

Yours sincerely,

James A. McCaughan.

(James A. McCaughan)

PS. Here is your lovely photo back to use again!

REV TREVOR MAGOWAN

ST. JAMES'S MANSE, BALLYMONEY, CO ANTRIM.

Have you heard about the man who hadn't spoken to his wife for 7 years?
He said that he didn't want to interrupt her!

Perhaps you might prefer the story of the Minister who was being chauffeur-driven to a Wedding. His Reverence sat behind the chauffeur and as he wanted to ask a question he tapped the driver on the shoulder.
The driver hit the roof of the limousine and turned round as white as a sheet, "Oh I'm so sorry sir," he said, "You see I usually drive the hearse!"

Or from the late REV.R.J. MCILMOYLE (Dervock) the story of the woman who went to see him complaining that her husband was chasing after younger women.
Mr McIlmoyle pointed to his dog, lying happily on the rug. "Do you see that dog," he said. "He chases after bicycles but he can never catch them and even if he could, he wouldn't know what to do with them!"

THE METHODIST CHURCH IN IRELAND
Secretary of Conference Rev. Edmund T. I. Mawhinney
1 Fountainville Avenue, Belfast BT9 6AN Tel: (0232) 324554

A man and his wife who lived in a rural part of Ulster had been unhappy with each other for most of their married life. There had been many squabbles and fights.

The husband died and unfortunately did not leave his affairs in good order with the result that the family had many disagreements over the farm and other possessions.

One day a neighbour said to the widow: 'If Tommy came back down again he would be very upset to see the way you're all fighting among each other'

'Well, indeed, he'll not come down' says the widow, 'for he never went up in the first place'

....

To prove his love for her, he swam the deepest river, crossed the widest desert, and climbed the highest mountain. She left him. He was never at home!

....

Before marriage he talks and she listens
After marriage she talks and he listens
Later they both talk and the neighbours listen.

....

Marriage begins when you sink in his arms and ends with your arms in the sink.

....

A minister in his speech at the wedding reception reminded all present that the newly married couple would be setting up a new home. He took the letter 'H' and spoke for about 10 minutes on the need for happiness in the home. He took another 10 minutes saying it was necessary to have Order in the home. Then he dealt with 'M' and spoke for another 10 minutes on management of the home. The letter 'E' he said stood for expenditure and lectured them for a further 10 minutes on financial affairs in their marriage.

After this 40 minutes talk, one guest was overheard saying to another:
'Thank goodness, they're not moving into a bungalow'

REV. C. R. J. RUDD

THE RECTORY,
MOIRA,
CRAIGAVON.
BT67 OLE

A nosey lady met a young woman,
"Well, how are you?"
"Not so bad!"
"That's good."
"I got married since I last met you,"
"That's good."
"Well, it's not so good - he's Very old,"
"Oh! That's bad."
"Well, it's not so bad - he's Very rich."
"That's good."
"Well it's not so good - he's Very miserable."
"Oh! That's bad."
"Oh! it's not so bad - he built me a beautiful bungalow on the hill."
"Oh! that's good."
"Well, its not so good, it got burned."
"Oh! That's bad."
"Well, it's not so bad - HE WAS IN IT!"

Duneane Presbyterian Church

(Fulton Memorial)

Duneane Manse
Randalstown
Antrim
BT41 3HZ

26th April 1990

REV. T. POLLOCK

"I'll never ask another woman to marry me as long as I live."
"Refused again?"
"No -- accepted."

INQUISITIVE SON: "Father which is the unluckiest month of the year to get married in?"
FATHER: "I don't know my boy. Everyone has to find that out for himself -- just as I did."

Heard about the man who said he did not know what happiness was until he got married and then he was too late.

REV E. J. MCKIMMON

LONDONDERRY

The parish priest was leaving his parish to go to Rome to do a special job at the Vatican. He called to say farewell to all his people.

He came to Bridget's house: "How have you been, Bridget, it is ten years since I married you and John." "Yes" said Bridget, "indeed it is and we are very happy, but have no children." "Well" said Father Pat, "never worry, Bridget, when I go to Rome I will light a candle for you."

Many years later Father Pat retired and the Pope said, "Why not go back to Ireland and visit your parish?" So Father Pat came and called on his friends. He came to Bridget's house: "well, how have you been, Bridget?" "Fine, Father Pat", said Bridget, "we now have fourteen of a family". "And", said Father Pat, "how is John doing?" "Oh" said Bridget,"he has gone off to Rome to blow out the candle!"

St. Dorothea's Parish Church, Gilnahirk

Church of Ireland

Rev John McKegney

St. Dorothea's Rectory,
237 Lower Braniel Road
Gilnahirk
Belfast BT5 7NQ

Dear Elizabeth,

Sorry for not relying to your letter long ago. I hope my story is not too late for your book of 'Wedding Humour'. It is an excellent idea and I would find a copy very useful.

with my best wishes
yours sincerely

John W McKegney

THE CHURCH BELLS
(Names can be changed to suit!)

Sam and Susan had been to a party. He asked to leave her home. She was lovely, he thought and she thought he was a bit of a hunk!

He asked to leave her home and as he did so they heard church bells ringing
"Why are the church bells ringing" said Susan
"Because, to-night, I have met the loviest girl in the world, and all the world is happy." answered Sam and they kissed!

Months passed and they fell more and more in love and one night he popped the question. Again they heard the bells ringing.
"Why are the church bells ringing" said Susan, again
"Because to-night they share our happiness as I have become engaged to the best girl in the word." said he, and they kissed.

More time passed and as they came out from their wedding the church bells were ringing and she asked the usual question, ""Why are the church bells ringing". Sam looked lovingly into her eyes and said "They are ringing for my lovely bride - all the world is happy." And they kissed.

Just over a year later they were out walking along, pushing a pram when they again heard the bells ringing and Susan again said, ""Why are the church bells ringing". He looked at their lovely little baby and said "They are ringing to share our joy as our first child is born" And they kissed.

Two more babies were to follow. The same questions were asked, the same answers given and they kissed each time. Many years passed and the children grew up and in time moved into homes of their own.

Sam and Susan went out for a walk one evening and they heard the church bells ringing, "Why are the church bells ringing" said Susan, again!
And Sam said "Because there's a team of men up the tower pulling the ropes, and it's time we were getting home"

So don't let romance die in your marriage, and don't keep asking the same questions.!

Rev S Eaton

PORTBALLINTRAE

A young pair went to see their minister one evening to make arrangements for their wedding. After completing and signing the necessary notice of marriage form the young prospective bridegroom asked the minister if he himself was married. The reply was No, but he added that he had been engaged at one time. "What happened", asked the young bridegroom. "Well", said the minister, "one evening I was out walking with my bride to be and a black cat happened to pass between us and we considered this a rather evil omen and we called the whole thing off." The young bridegroom asked "Was that all that really happened." "Yes, that's all", replied the minister. "Well theres only one thing I can say to that", remarked the young bridegroom,

"If I had been in your place I would have been so close to her that no black cat could have passed between us."

Good advice to young married couples - Watch the black cats, .. especially the two legged ones!

Hazelbank Presbyterian Church

HAZELBANK ROAD, COLERAINE.

Minister:
REV SAMUEL JOHN MILLAR, M.A
THE MANSE
4 Knocklayde Park,
Coleraine, BT51 3HW
Telephone: 52891

Clerk of Session:
WILLIAM JOHNSTON
6 Altmore Park,
Coleraine, BT51 3NP
Telephone, 58459

Hon. Secretary:
HUGH J. GUY
26 Mountsandel Road,
Coleraine, BT52 1JE
Telephone: 51441

Monday 22nd January 1990.

An advertisement in the Irish Farmers Journal read like this:-

"Bachelor Farmer from the West of Ireland, with good going thresher seeks a strong healthy spinster with a good going tractor, with view to marriage".

P.S Please send photo of Tractor

An old bachelor in the Highlands, decided at last to get married and his minister, said, "Donald I trust you have got a hand maid of the Lord. "Indeed minister", said Donald.

"I dinna ken whether she's hand-made or machine made, but she's gay weel put together".

REV DAVID ALDERDICE

21 Old Galgorm Rd
BALLYMENA

Young woman wakened up screaming in the middle of the night, "What's wrong, dear?"
"Oh" - she said, "I had a terrible dream.
"Tell me about it", he said.
"Well, I was at an auction - It was an auction of husbands."
"How were they going?" he asked.
"Well, good husbands were going at 5,000 pounds, and ordinary husbands were going at 2,000 pounds.
"And what about husbands like me", he asked.
"Oh thats why I was screaming, they were tying them up in bundles of 50 and selling them at 5p a bundle."

REV CANON F.W. FAWCETT M.A.

The Rectory
Newtown Street
STRABANE
Co Tyrone

SHARING IN MARRIAGE

John and Mary just recently married, decided that they would share everything.

It would be Our House, Our Motorcar, Our Furniture, and indeed Our Cat.

One night as they lay in bed Mary heard a knocking on their front door. She nudged John saying "Get up, there is someone at the door. No reply! She tried a second time, with this reply. "Mary dear, where is OUR TROUSERS!

Second Presbyterian Church, Comber

Minister: The Rev. PAUL ERSKINE, M.A., B.D.
The Manse, 5 Killinchy Street, Comber, Newtownards, BT23 5AP. Telephone 872261

10th May 1990

Dear Jillian,

Thank you for your letter. My favourite wedding joke is about the bridegroom who was extremely nervous. He was shaking so much that he couldn't stand still for photographs and only with difficulty could stutter out his vows. When he came to sign the register, his hand shook so much that the pen made no imprint on the paper. The clergyman said to him, "Put your weight on it." The bridegroom signed, "John Smith 10½ stone"!

All good wishes in your endeavours to raise funds for your Church.

Yours sincerely,

Paul Erskine

Rev. Paul Erskine

REV GEORGE SLEATH
12 Queen's Ave
BALLYMONEY
Co Antrim

The bride was having difficulty with the word "OBEY" during the marriage ceremony. All she could manage to say was "bey" even though encouraged by the Minister to pronounce the word properly.

Finally, the bridegroom could stand it no longer, "Leave her to me your Reverence", he said "I'll make her say "OH" when we get home."

Rev. William Nicholl
Tel.: (0265) 822255

2 CORRSTOWN PARK
HOPEFIELD ROAD
PORTRUSH BT56
Co. ANTRIM
N. IRELAND

20.1.90

Some people collect epitaphs or sayings taken from tombstones in church yards. Such sayings can be very memobable or humorous. Take the one found on the tomb of a husband and wife who had been married for 40 years : "Their warfare is accomplished".

REV CANON R M WILKINSON
60 Coleraine Road
PORTRUSH

A red Indian Chief decided that one wife wasn't enough for somebody in such an important position as himself, and so he married three girls at the same time.

He took them back to his tent, and pointed out the sleeping quarters to them.
The first of his wives was to sleep on a buffalo skin, the second on a hippopotamus skin and the third on an antelope skin.

In time the wife who slept on the buffalo skin gave birth to a baby boy; the wife who slept on the hippopotamus skin gave birth to twins, a boy and a girl; and the wife who slept on the antelope skin gave birth to a baby girl.

This proves that the squaw on the hippopotamus is equal to the sum of the squaws on the other two hides.

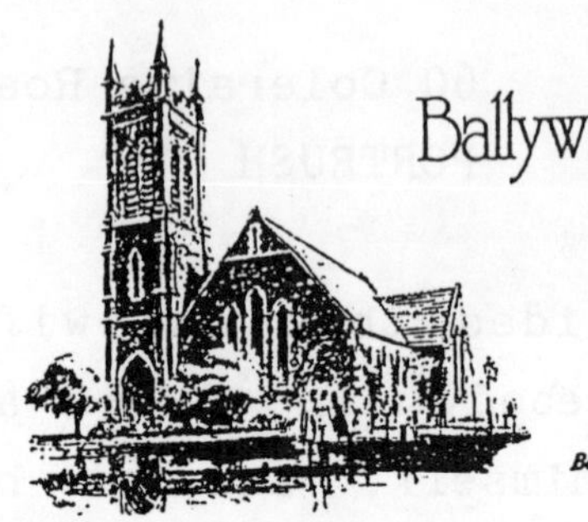

Ballywillan Presbyterian Church

Portrush, Co. Antrim.

Minister: Rev. James Frazer,
Ballywillan Manse, 95 Gateside Road, Portrush BT56 8NP

A country couple were courting, and they were doing it so loudly that all the neighbours were able to hear. Eventually everybody got tired of it, and complained to the couple.

"Can you not do that quietly?"

"Well", the fellow said,

"We have to do it back to back, for we are both of different religions, and neither of us will turn!"

THE CORRYMEELA COMMUNITY

REV DOUG BAKER

A true story from a wedding I attended several years ago. The bride had invited a priest she had worked with several years before that to come and give the address. He accepted but wasn't sure just what his role was, since he was not actually officiating at the wedding.

So he asked her what exactly she wanted him to do. She said, "Just keep it short. Just give your address when it's time and then sit down again - that's all you have to do."

When the time did come he stood up, repeated the bride's instructions to him, said this was her day and so he would obey them. Then he said, "So here is my address:

168 Bayswater Road, London, W3," and then sat down.

The congregation waited, the bride waited - but he sat. That was what she had asked him to do and that was what he did - gave his address and sat down.

After a long embarrassing and then funny pause, she turned to him and said "Oh, get up and say whatever you want to" - and he then gave a splendid wedding address.

REV. W. R. LINDSAY

THE MANSE CROSSMORE ROAD KEADY

Peggy was an old maid who lived alone, she was very lonely, she kept her house spick and span hoping that one day she would get a husband. She did not know if it would be wrong to pray for one but she kept on hoping.

One lovely evening she sat down under an apple tree, to do her wishing. Up above her on a branch sat an owl. Suddenly it called out "who? who? who?" Peggy all excited thinking it was an answer to her bequest shouted at the top of her voice, "Oh I am not particular, any old man would do!"

Lizzie was an old maid, who had been quite good looking in her young days, but never managed to get a husband. A new Minister was coming to a neighbouring church, he was a bachelor about fifty years old. Lizzie at once was determined to catch him. Decked in her best and with all the modern beauty aids applied, set out early and went into the back seat of the church.

On the wall above her was the barometer. The Minister and sexton appeared at the far end of the church talking. The sexton then came down and stopped before her to look at the barometer, he shouted back to the Minister, "She's over sixty." Up jumped Lizzie out of the door as fast as she could, thinking it was her that was over sixty.

Waterside Presbyterian Church

Minister: Rev. J. M. CATHCART, M.A.

8 Altnagelvin Park,
Londonderry.
BT47 2LU
Telephone: 48155

22nd Feb. 90

Dear Jillian

I am pleased to have the opportunity to include the funny statement below in your book "Wedding Humour". I wish you well and hope that when the book is published you will let me buy a copy; I'm always on the look-out for funny Wedding Stories.

-o-o-o-o-o-

" Marriage is like the Bath! After you are in it for a while, it's not so hot."

-o-o-o-o-o-

This is not true but I think it's funny.

With best wishes,

Maynard Cathcart

Carnlough Presbyterian Church

59 BAY ROAD
CARNLOUGH
BALLYMENA
BT44 0HJ

Rev. R. S. ROSS
Phone: (0574) 85268

The bride and bridegroom were being photographed at the front of the church. They were standing beside the Church Notice Board on which was the text -

"Father, forgive them for they know not what they do."

"FATHER, FORGIVE
THEM, FOR THEY
KNOW NOT WHAT
THEY DO."

GIRL GUIDES

(INCORPORATED BY ROYAL CHARTER)

Methodist Church Hall,
Queen Street,
Coleraine.

Dear Reverend. T. Magowan,

I am writing to ask if you would be so kind as to tell me the best or funniest wedding story or wedding joke that you know.

My two friends and I, who are members of the 7th Coleraine Guide Company, would like to compile a book entitled 'Wedding Humour', and donate the proceeds to our church's restoration fund which needs £150 000.

Please help us.

Yours sincerely,

Elizabeth Simmons.

Aged 14.

THE METHODIST CHURCH IN IRELAND

COLERAINE, PORTRUSH, PORTSTEWART & BALLYMONEY CIRCUIT

REV. T. MAGOWAN 33 Grange Road
COLERAINE

The caretaker was chatting to the Minister in the vestry after the bridal party had left the church. "Did you ever see such an ugly bride your reverence?" said the caretaker.
"Now, now, James", replied the Minister, "remember she is God's handiwork."
"That may be so but she certainly is not His masterpiece!"

A young woman went to the Dole Office and because she could not read or write, was in the habit of signing for her money with a "X". Then one day she came in and signed the usual form with a "Y".
"Why did you not make your usual "X"? inquired the girl behind the counter. "I suppose you haven't heard," she said, "but last week I got married and I've changed my name."

The young bride and groom had a quarrel and had not spoken for hours. Suddenly the man saw a donkey in a field, "relative of yours?" he asked.
"Yes", the young bride replied "by marriage."

BALLYEASBORO RECTORY
187 MAIN ROAD
PORTAVOGIE, NEWTOWNARDS
Co. DOWN, BT22 1DA
TEL: PORTAVOGIE (0247) 71234

REV.F.W.A.BELL

Mark and Joan had recently been married and went to live next door to an older couple called John and Jane. Each morning at 7.45 the men set off to catch the 8 a.m. train for their work.

Jane would rise early and make John's breakfast, collect his papers and his bag and usher him towards the door making sure that he would not be late for the train. Both men would bid their wives goodbye at the door at the same time each morning. Jane would wave goodbye to her husband but Mark and Joan would linger on the doorstep hugging and kissing each other.

One morning, Jane observing the activity of the young couple next door and feeling a little jealous, called her husband back and said to him, "Do you not see the way the young couple next door say goodbye as they part each morning. Could you not do the same thing?"

"How could I" said John. "Sure I don't know the girl well enough!"

The Most Reverend Anthony Farquhar

Titular Bishop of Ermiana

73a Somerton Road,
Belfast. BT15 4DE

Telephones 773935 / 776185

From the office of the Auxiliary Bishops of Down and Connor

9th May, 1990.

Miss Elizabeth Simmons
7th Coleraine Guides,
Methodist Church Hall,
Queen Street,
COLERAINE.

Dear Elizabeth,

I apologise for the delay in replying to your letter of 10th April but I have been away quite a bit at meetings, on parish visitations and officiating at Confirmation ceremonies.

I hope that the enclosed will be of use to you and that your book 'Wedding Humour' will raise a substantial sum towards your church's restoration fund.

With every best wish.

Yours sincerely,

+Anthony J Farquhar

A bridegroom who was a keen football supporter was upset that his wedding coincided with his team playing a vital cup tie. During the reception he kept inquiring if the waiter knew the score. When finally informed that his team had won 3-1, he said: "Oh it has not been such a bad day after all".

TOBERKEIGH PRESBYTERIAN CHURCH

MINISTER
REV. IAN McCLEAN
134 Moycraig Road.
Ballyoglagh.
Ballymoney.
BT53 8QZ.
Tel: Dervock (02657) 41798

CLERK OF SESSION
MR. JAMES CHESTNUTT
9 Clougher Road.
Clougher South.
Bushmills.
BT57 8XP.
Tel: Bushmills (02657) 31698

SECRETARY
MR. DANIEL KANE
Ballinlea House.
68 Ballinlea Road.
Ballycastle.
BT54 6JL.
Tel: Ballycastle (02657) 62678

REV.IAN McCLEAN

A young man approached his wise old bachelor uncle with a problem. He had a choice of two women. One was a middle-aged widow, plain looking, but with a good farm of land, well stocked, and with a fair bank balance.
The other was young, beautiful and penniless.
What would he do?

The uncle's advice was immediate "Tak' the young yin!" He did, and life was blissful.

Sometime later he approached his uncle thanking him for the good advice, and asking if there was any way he could ever repay him for the good turn.
There was, "Could ye gimme t'address o' thon widda?"

Cregagh Presbyterian Church

Rev. Albert A. Sleith M.A., B.Ed.,
(Minister)
Telephone 798348

11 Kensington Gardens
Belfast BT5 6NP

21st March 1990

Husband and wife married for 10 years one day playing golf. His wife at the 13th hole says "John, if I died would you marry again?"
"Well, hum um um, I might" he replies, "I'm only 35 years old."
"Tell me John would you bring her to live in our house?"
"Well", said John, "If I do marry again, I suppose I would."
"Would she wear my jewellery?" etc. "Would she sleep in our bed?"
"Well I suppose so".
"John would she play with my golf clubs?"
"Definitely not," said John.
"But why?"
"Because she is left handed."

John, "My wife is an angel, Sammy."
Sammy, "You're lucky, my wife is still alive."

1ST PRESBYTERIAN CHURCH

ARMAGH

REV W.J. SLEITH

Marriage is like a three ring circus

First the ENGAGEMENT RING

Then the WEDDING RING

Then the S U F F E R I N G

REVD. CANON DR. C. THORNTON, PHD., B.D., LTH.

PORTRUSH

THE FAMILY BUSINESS

Two bachelor brothers, Mick and Dick lived together on their remote farm One day, Mick said: "I think I'll get married and bring a wife home here."

Dick: "Surely you would never do that."

Mick: "Why not?"

Dick: "Because you and I could never discuss family business in front of a stranger."

Very Rev. Canon Hugh P. Murphy

O.B.E., R.D., P.P.

---

305 Shore Road
NEWTOWNABBEY

Clergyman examines children:-

1) What law or commandment would you break if you disobey your parents?

2) What law or commandment..... if you stole money?

3) What law or commandment would you break if you caught a cat by the tail and whirled it round your head till the tail came off?

Answer "WHAT GOD HAS JOINED TOGETHER MAN MUST NOT PULL ASUNDER."

REV CECIL J JAMISON

2 Leighinmohr Park
BALLYMENA
BT42 2AW

There was a famous case of a young man, Basil Ne-mas in Da-maly on the Black Sea. Now according to a press report! Absolutely true this, in 1972, Basil fell passionately in love with his neighbour's daughter.

But unfortunately his affection was spurned. Not to be defeated, however, Basil Ne-mas decided he would do the romantic thing and sweep the young lady off her feet with a classic lover's abduction.

So soon after midnight this intrepid (undaunted) young lover arrived in his beloved's garden armed with a ladder. He climbed into her room, threw a blanket over her sleeping form, carried her down to his car whispering tender endearments in the end of the blanket where you might reasonably expect her ears to have been!

Away they sped into the night, joy in his heart, stars in the sky, all that kind of thing.

However, when he unwrapped his precious cargo, pursed his lips for a kiss, he discovered to his astonishment it was in fact the girl's granny, 91 years old! Who had never liked him! Who took the welcome opportunity to beat him about the head so severely that he was hospitalized and that's where the reporter found him!

REV J.E.P.BOYD

TERRACE ROW PRESBYTERIAN CHURCH,

COLERAINE

This is the advice given by the Minister to the bridegroom at the Wedding Reception.

Lifting a knife the Minister declared,
"See and carve a way through life for your wife."

Lifting a spoon he advised,
"See and keep up the spooning."

Finally, lifting up a fork he told the bridegroom,
"And don't forget to fork out your pay to your wife every week."

REV.T.A.B.SAWYERS

"Lynwood,"
82 Coleraine Road
PORTRUSH

Some years ago my wife had a group of ladies in the rectory for supper. During the evening she passed round a tray of chocolates. Each guest took a chocolate, but one rather figure conscious lady. She refused saying - "You see this chocolate, (holding it between her two fingers) it would be on my lips for seconds and my hips for years.

A prominent leader of the Mother's Union addressed some two hundred members on the subject - "Making Husbands Happy."
She spoke at length about warm homes, slippers at the ready, favourite food, quiet children, love and lots of it.
Finally, totally satisfied with the reception her talk received from the audience, she rather foolishly asked the members to stand up all who wished to MOTHER their husbands. Only one lady got to her feet. "I'm shocked" she said, "Only one person going to mother her husband."
"I beg your pardon Madam", said the lady who had stood up, and whose husband had a well known gambling problem, "I thought you said SMOTHER him."

HOUSE OF COMMONS
LONDON SW1A 0AA

1st. June, 1990.

Miss Elizabeth Simmons,
7th Coleraine Guides,
Methodist Church Hall,
Queen Street,
Coleraine.

Dear Elizabeth,

Thank you for your letter concerning your great idea of compiling a book on "Wedding Humour".

I remember once hearing a story about a young lady called Jayne Lemon, and a young man called Ebenezer Sweet, who decided to get married. At their wedding a poem was read out that went something like this:

"Behold what strong extremes do meet, in Jayne and Ebenezer.
Jayne has changed her name to sweet, but Eb's a lemon squeezer."

I hope you are able to use this little poem in your book.

Yours sincerely,

P.P. Ian Paisley
IAN R. K. PAISLEY M.P., M.E.P.

REV ISAAC COLE

118 COLERAINE RD
PORTRUSH

A young man from East Belfast called with his Minister to make arrangements for his wedding.

The Minister proceeded to complete the marriage forms and one of the questions he asked the young man was - "Is the young lady a Spinster?"

The young man replied "No, she is a Hemstitcher."

Rev B H S Liddell, M.A.

CASTLEROCK

Two cannibals, having a meal, were talking to each other.

One said, "I didn't like my Mother-in-Law."

The other said "Don't bother with her, just eat the chips."

The Deanery,
30 Bishop Street,
Londonderry,
BT48 6PP
Telephone: 262746.

21st March 1990

Dear Gillian

Thank you for you letter. Here is a funny Wedding story -

'An old man was asked what was the secret of his long and healthy life. He said that when he and his wife got married they agreed that if she ever got angry and started to scold him he would go out into the farmyard until she quietened down. If ever he got roused about anything she would do the same. 'And do you know this,' he said ' I've spent most of my life in the open air! That's why I'm so healthy.'

I hope this is of some help to you. I would love to have a copy of the book when published.

Yours sincerely

D C ORR
DEAN

REV.J.C.PARKE

143 Mill Road
PORTSTEWART

I frequently tell the assembled guests that

"A good wife halves her husband's sorrows, doubles his joys, and trebles his expenses."

also -

"A good wife saves her husband half the troubles a bachelor never knows."

PARISH OF ST CLEMENT, BELFAST

REV. J. STEWART

St Clement's
Sandown Road
BELFAST

The Minister was delayed getting to the church. The bride and groom on this occasion had to do the waiting. The Minister eventually arrived, conducted the wedding service and the couple went off to the wedding reception.

About 10 years later the Minister met the man again and said to him, "do you remember the fright I gave you on your Wedding day?"
"I do indeed, the man replied, and she is still with me."

Glendermott Parish Church

The Rev. R. N. MOORE, M.A.

Tel. Londonderry 43001

Glendermott Rectory,
Altnagelvin.
Londonderry BT47 2LS

21.3 1990

The Rev.R.N.Moore, M.A.

Three sisters talking about marriage:-

I WILL MARRY

(1) A DOCTOR because he will cure me for nothing.

(2) A FARMER because he will feed me for nothing.

(3) A Clergyman because he will make me Good FOR NOTHING.

Honeymoon Salad = LET US ALONE (LETTUCE)

Rev R. Desmond Morris

Dunmurry, Belfast

The young bridal pair almost missed their honeymoon flight, and unfortunately, at the last minute, could not get two seats together. A short time after the plane was on its course, the bride, feeling somewhat lonely wrote a love note to her newly-wed. It ran: "I think you are very handsome and attractive. Would you care to join me for an unforgettable evening!"? The lady in seat number 4C.

The stewardess kindly delivered her note and a little later returned with a refreshing drink of juice and said, "The man in seat 16C was really flattered, but said he must decline your generous offer because he was on his honeymoon."

When the journey was over and the bride and groom were together again she said to him, "Thank you so much for the welcome drink you gave me on the 'plane."
"But," he said, all surprised, "I didn't send you one". He had been sitting in seat number 14C!!

University of Ulster at Coleraine   Coleraine Co. Londonderry BT52 1SA Northern Ireland

REVEREND J.E.G. BACH JP BA Dipl Th.

The Chaplaincy,
70 Hopefield Ave.
PORTRUSH

WEDDING JOKE

It is in the form of a toast for the bride and groom, and it goes:

"I wish you the wisdom of Solomon, the patience of Job, and the children of Israel."

Father Brian Mullan

1, Seafield Park South
PORTSTEWART

Arriving at the church to attend a wedding, the woman was tackled by the Usher.

"Are you a friend of the groom, madam?"

"Certainly not", she replied I'm the bride's mother!"

REV J N GOULDEN

BALLYCASTLE

When I came to Belfast, after ordination, in 1941 during the war I was shy and bashful. To get to know the parishioners required a lot of visiting and as I was from the west of Ireland I found it hard to make conversation. I called at this house one day to have the door opened by a blushing girl. I introduced myself and she asked me in. Sitting on the settee was a soldier who looked ill at ease on seeing me, a clergyman. She sat down beside him and blushed more. Conversation was very restrained as I did not know what to say to them or they to me. After some vain attempts I decided to leave, and as a parting farewell gesture I said "When is the big day" and literally made my escape.

I had forgotten the incident when one night a few weeks later in the blackout the door bell rang. Here were the couple standing in the hallway and I asked them in. "I did not think I'd see you again" said I. The soldier replied "I got three day leave in order to come and propose to N... I spent two days trying to pluck up enough courage to propose and failed. I had only two hours left before I had to rejoin my unit. But after what you said I got courage and proposed and N accepted and we want you to marry us." We arranged the date and I had the pleasure of performing the ceremony.

From: The Dean of Belfast. Very Revd. Jack Shearer.
The Deanery, 5 Deramore Drive. Belfast BT9 5JQ.
Tel. 0232 660980.

Dear Elizabeth,

here is a good cartoon which you could use.

Best Wishes
Jack Shearer

"Well wake him."

CASTLEROCK, DUNBOE AND FERMOYLE UNION OF PARISHES

DIOCESE OF DERRY

The Rev. W. Brian Johnston, M.A.

The Rectory,
52 Main Street,
Castlerock,
Co. Londonderry.
BT51 4RA

22nd January 1990

Dear Jillian,

Your letter of 15th January set me a real problem. As you can imagine I hear so many Wedding jokes and many so often that they no longer seem as funny as when I first heard them. One of my favourites is as follows.

A certain man always said that he would remain a bachelor for ever. He enjoyed the company of many ladies and could see no reason to tie himself to just one. As each of his friends got married he teased them mercilessly and always found a new practical joke to play on each.

However, like many others eventually he found a girl that he wanted to marry and the arrangements were made. As the day approached he got more and more nervous and warned his bride that he felt that his friends were ganging up to really get him. His friends just smiled and said that the best joke for them was that he had eventually been caught. They all intended going to the wedding so that he could not chicken out.

The day of the wedding arrived and nothing had happened so he began to relax. Then at the beginning of the Service, when the Minister said 'If any man can show any just cause why they may not lawfully be joined together, let him now speak,' a voice from the back of the Church said 'Stop the wedding'. As the Minister, the Bride and Groom watched, a very well dressed man that they did not know walked forward.

He reached the front, looked at the Bride, looked at the Groom, looked at the Minister, looked round them all again and then said 'Sorry, wrong wedding' and walked out of the Church.

Good luck in your project, I hope you get many better jokes than this and that your book is a success. I am returning your photograph as I am sure there is some younger gentleman (boyfriend) who would just love to have it.

With best wishes,

W. Brian Johnston

Bishop's House
St. Eugene's Cathedral
Derry BT48 9AP
Ireland

Tel. Derry (0504) 262302
Fax No. (0504) 371960

March 20, 1990

Miss Jillian Boyd
13 Cairnmount Road
COLERAINE BT51 3JR

Dear Jillian

Thank you for your lovely letter and photograph which I received at the weekend.

This is a true story of a wedding which took place many years ago long before I was appointed as bishop . . .

After the wedding ceremony in the church, I went to a wedding reception in an hotel. I arrived a little late and I sat down at a table just inside the door of the reception room. There was silence at the table - nothing to be heard but the rattle of knives and forks; obviously the bride's friends and groom's friends had not met. They were strangers to one another.

One man, about two places from me, obviously wished to break the ice - he coughed and fidgeted - and then he said to the lady opposite - "How is your mother keeping?". The lady opposite answered quickly, "She died six months ago!".

After that, the silence was even greater than before!

I then looked up at the top table - I had never seen the bride and groom in my life before! Only then did I realise I was at the right hotel but the wrong reception. My wedding was in another room in the same hotel!

I politely excused myself and went to the other reception. I do not know if the guests at the other reception eventually got around to having a conversation.

I hope that this is what you require and wish you success in your efforts to compile your book and raise funds for your church's restoration fund.

Yours sincerely

+ Edward Daly

Bishop of Derry

REV E. J. MCKIMMON

LONDONDERRY

A minister called to see a husband and wife who had been quarrelling. He had been asked to go and see them to 'have a word'! He listened to both sides of the story but seemed to be getting nowhere. Then he noticed the cat and the dog lying stretched out beside each other in front of the fire. "Look", he said, "the cat and the dog can live together in harmony and affection". "Yes!" said the husband, but tie the two of them together and see what happens!"

PARISH *of* GLENCRAIG

Vicar: The Revd. Canon Alwyn Maconachie, M.A., B.D., R.D.

Clergyman (or friend) "My final advice to the Groom for a happy marriage is - always be the head of the house."
And to the bride - you - always be the neck that turns the head!"

METHODIST CHURCH IN IRELAND

(Glastry and Portaferry Circuit)

Superintendent Minister :
Rev. W. A. AGNEW, B.A.
20 Victoria Road.
Ballyhalbert, Newtownards.
Co. Down. BT22 1DG.
Tel : Kircubbin 210

Rev W.A. Agnew, B.A.,

A young couple anxious to have an unusual honeymoon decided to tour Ireland in a horse and trap. They took a wad of notes with them as ready cash for the journey. They were held up by robbers who took everything including the horse and trap.

The husband said to the wife, "We have no money, what are we going to do?"
She replied, "When I saw them coming I put the wad of notes into my mouth. They didn't notice it so here they are."
He replied, "You're clever, Mary, What a pity your mother wasn't with us. If she had been here we could have saved the horse and trap as well."

Ara Coeli
Ard Mhacha/Armagh

May 1, 1990.

Dear Elizabeth,

Thank you for your letter of 10th April. I am sorry for the delay in replying to it as I was abroad for some time since Easter.

I hope your two friends and yourself receive many wedding stories for your book and I am happy to send a little contribution which I hope will be suitable.

Thank you for sending me such a happy photograph of yourself. You have obviously a keen sense of humour and I am sure that the collection of 'Wedding Humour' which you will put together will be very enjoyable.

Yours very sincerely,

S.J. Clyne

p.p. Cardinal Archbishop of Armagh
(dictated by Cardinal Ó Fiaich and signed in his absence by the Diocesan Secretary)

Miss Elizabeth Simmons,
3 Apollo Crescent,
PORTRUSH,
Co. Antrim,
BT56 8SA.

Wedding Stories

1. Husband boasting on the Golden Jubilee of his Wedding:

   "Some people ask me for the secret of our very happy marriage. The secret is that we have always taken time off to dine out twice a week. You can imagine how the relaxed meal, the soft music and the dancing by candlelight made the evenings out very enjoyable. She went out on Tuesdays and I went out on Fridays".

2. "I went into marriage", said the regretful husband, "with my two eyes closed - one closed by her father and the other closed by her brother".

3. Someone has said that Marriage is a drama in three acts.

   In the first act, which is the courtship, he talks and she listens.

   In the second act, which is the honeymoon, she talks and he listens.

   In the third act, which begins after the honeymoon, the two of them talk and the neighbours listen.

Ballylaggan Reformed Presbyterian Church

Rev. W.D.J. McKAY, B.A., B.D., M.Th.
82 Curragh Road, Aghadowey, Coleraine, BT51 4BS.
Telephone: Aghadowey 868233

Two cannibals were walking through the jungle - a cannibal father and his cannibal son. Suddenly they saw a beautiful girl walking along in front of them. The son got very excited and asked his father, "Will we take her home and eat her?"

The cannibal father answered, "Son, you have a lot to learn. Take her home and eat your mother!"

<u>REV.J.PATTON TAYLOR</u>

The Manse
Duncairn Avenue,
<u>BELFAST</u> BT14 6BP

"YOU CAN LOOK FORWARD TO VISITS FROM MOTHER-IN-LAW. SHE ALWAYS COMES TO STAY WHEN HER BROOMSTICK IS IN FOR SERVICING."

THE BISHOP OF CONNOR
Rt. Rev. S. G. Poyntz, B.D., Ph.D.

Bishop's House,
22 Deramore Park,
Belfast BT9 5JU.
Telephone: 668442

Date 19 March 1990

Miss J. Boyd
13 Cairnmount Park
COLERAINE
County Londonderry
BT51 3 JR.

Dear Jillian,

Thank you for your letter concerning stories for your book entitled "Wedding Humour". I greatly hope that the following may be of some help:

(1) Kevin, a cockney lad, couldn't make up his mind which girl to marry. Sharon had blonde hair and blue eyes, Maria had black hair and green eyes. Sharon had a quick tongue, but she was funny, Maria was sweet-natured and serious. Over and over again he compared the two girls. The trouble was, both of them loved him and he loved both of them. One day, he was passing the Catholic church and although he wasn't very religious, he decided in desperation to go in and pray.
'Oh God', he cried, falling on his knees, 'Oo should I marry? I know I 'ave to make a choice, so 'elp me Lord. What d'yer say, Sharon or Maria, Maria or Sharon?'
Then the miracle occurred. He looked up and there above the altar, in letters of gold, was the advice, 'AVE MARIA'. So he did.

(2) A woman who took her husband 'for better, for worse' found that he proved to be far worse then she took him for.

(3) A free-church clergyman was so scrupulous about his morals that he refused to perform any marriage ceremonies. His conscience would not allow him to participate in any game of chance.

All good wishes for your publication.

Yours sincerely,

+ Samuel Connor:

+ Samuel Connor:

The Very Rev. Ronald G. Craig, B.A., D.D.

BUSHMILLS

One against myself was on a Saturday when I had five weddings, one every hour. I knew the words backwards and it became rather monotonous, but I must almost have been in a trance when in the last ceremony instead of saying, "Forasmuch as John and Mary have covenanted ... I declare them to be husband and wife. I found myself saying "Forasmuch as it hath pleased Almighty God to take unto himself the soul of ...." These are the words from the burial service and it was beyond me to turn the sentence round to suit a marriage declaration!

Brides and grooms like to have their favourite hymns, whether suitable or not.
I remember my young organist coming to me rather perturbed. The bride wanted to have the hymn, "Abide with me, fast falls the eventide, the darkness deepens." He did not think this very suitable. Neither did I!

Coleraine Parish

Rector: Rev. Kenneth H. Clarke,
St. Patrick's Rectory,
Mountsandel Road,
Coleraine BT52 1JE.
Telephone: 3429

23rd January, 1990.

Dear Jillian,

Thank you very much indeed for your letter, for your beautiful photograph and for the invitation to share with you one of the funniest wedding stories that I know.

The story is as follows:-

There is a rumour going round that in the Church of Ireland it is possible for one man to have 16 wives. Some argue this is what our Church of Ireland Prayer Book teaches. However, when the rumour was investigated, it was discovered some one had misunderstood what a Rector had said in the marriage service. The listener thought he had said in the service, "Four better, four worse, four richer, four poorer". I hasten to add that in the Church of Ireland there is one man, one wife and their marriage is for better, for worse, for richer, for poorer.

I trust that this story will be useful, Jillian and I wish you every success in the writing of your book 'Wedding Humour'.

Yours sincerely,

Ken Clarke

Rev K Gregg
COLERAINE

Scene: Farmyard - November Evening

John the ploughman has finished work. He has closed down the byres and stables. The animals are fed and housed for the night. He lifts down the hurricane lamp from its hook at the Kitchen door and proceeds down the yard, homeward bound. As he is leaving the farmer meets him -
"John - where are you going tonight?"
"I'm going to see my Mary."
"Going Courting! - I didn't need the hurricane when I was going courting."

"No Sir - but look what you got!"

Overheard at Railway Station -

Wellwishers clapping the happy couple aboard
"They're all the one the noo."

"They maybe, but as far as the Railway Company is concerned, it will still take the twa tickets."

Rev K Gregg COLERAINE

SCENE: SON ENGAGED TO BE MARRIED - SEEKS FATHER'S ADVICE

"Dad, when I am married who will be boss?"

"Son, I tell you how you will find out - Visit all the farms and small holdings in the Parish, take with you six ponies and sixty hens. "Duly the young man set off and did as he was told. After many calls he still had six ponies, but he was fast running out of hens. Then it happened at a lovely little farm dwelling where the good woman was looking over her half door. She was pale and frail - "Who is the boss in this house?" - before she could answer a man's head appeared at her shoulder.

"I am", he said in a gruff voice.

"Is that so?" asked our young friend.

"Yes" came the meek reply "He is."

"Well then you can have the pick of these ponies. "Out came the man.

"This one - I think, but just a second."

He went over to the half door and man and wife spoke for a few minutes, both returned and she put her hand on a different animal.

"This one" he said.

"No, No, my dear chap, you will just have a hen."

ARCHDEACON G. W. A. KNOWLES

LIMAVADY

A minister, counselling a young lady, suggested that she start praying for others rather than for herself. That night her room-mate overheard her when she prayed: "O Lord, I am not asking anything for myself, but please give mother a son-in-law."

Hope your efforts are crowned with success. G.W.A. Knowles.

First Limavady Presbyterian Church

REV GEORGE D. SIMPSON

A man wondered what to buy his wife for Christmas. He decided to buy her a plot of ground in the local cemetery.

The following year he did not buy her anything, so she asked him,
"Why did you not buy me a Christmas present this year?"
"Well," he replied, "you did not use the one I bought you last year."

METHODIST CHURCH IN IRELAND
SPRINGFIELD AND CHURCH HILL CIRCUIT

REV JOHN J. WILSON — Church Hill Manse, ENNISKILLEN

TOAST TO THE UNMARRIED LADIES

"MAY THE LORD BLESS THEM AND KEEP THEM."

CANON STAFFORD
PREBENDARY OF TAPLESTONE

PRIMACY RECTORY
4 GLENDOWAN WAY
BANGOR
CO. DOWN BT19 2SP
TEL: (0247) 456625

In general it is true to say that a young man is incomplete until he's married; and when he is married, he's finished 'good and proper'.

My mother-in-law comes around for Christmas dinner at our house every year. Next year I think we'll better let her in.

The father of the Bride has this consolation - he may be losing a daughter but he's gaining a bathroom.

REV DAVID CUPPLES

8A Chanterhill Rd
ENNISKILLEN
BT74 6DE

When I was conducting my first wedding I was a bit nervous. I wanted to make it all very meaningful for the bride and groom. When it came to the vows, I should have kept my eyes on what I was reading since the bride and groom are meant to be speaking to each other. Instead I lifted my eyes and looked at them. I got the the groom's vows right but as the bride was repeating her vows after me she began to laugh. I suddenly realised I had asked her to say she would be a faithful and dutiful husband!

Last year I arrived in my room at the church and the groom and his best man were there. There was a terrible smell in the room, and I thought it was strong drink. I was a little worried but didn't like to ask.

Later on I discovered the answer. The best man was an artist, and travelling from East Germany some of his artist's materials had spilt on his clothes inside his travelling case. As a result the tie he was wearing at the wedding was smelling strongly of paint thinners!

Rev J. B. Mooney

BELFAST

CAKE GRITTY

New Bride: "How do you like my cake, dear?"

New Groom: "It tastes a bit gritty."

New Bride: "The recipe called for three eggs beaten up. Maybe I didn't beat the shells up small enough."

Revolving Door

Tom: "Where did you meet your girl friend?"

John: "I met her in a revolving door and we have been going around together ever since."

REV ROBERT S FISHER 22, Seafield Park
PORTSTEWART

A young lady had taken vows of poverty in a certain Convent. She inherited a sum of money on the death of an aunt. News of the legacy reached the Mother Superior. She was eventually called to the office of the Mother Superior who reminded her of the vows she had taken. You must go into the town and give it to the first poor person you meet. She obeyed and on going into town she met a poorly dressed man, with disevelled hair, bleary eyes, down at the heel appearance coming along.

She stopped him, put the money in his hand and said "God speed" and disappeared into the Convent. That night she answered the door bell. On opening the large door she was confronted with the same poor man.

He put a large sum of money into her hand and said, "God Speed won at 20 to one!

THE BRIDEGROOM HAS BACKED A WINNER.

Cregagh Presbyterian Church

Rev. Albert A. Sleith M.A., B.Ed.,
(Minister)
Telephone 798348

11 Kensington Gardens
Belfast BT5 6NP

21st March 1990

After a couple returned from their honeymoon, the husband replied to his wife's inquiry about what he would like for breakfast,

"Two eggs, one boiled and one fried."

Down he came for breakfast and his wife dutifully placed the two eggs on his plate. He began to sulk, "What's wrong dear?", she asked "there are your two eggs, one fried and one boiled, so what's the matter?"

"You fried the wrong one" he replied.

Upper Falls Rectory
28, Upper Green,
Dunmurry
BELFAST BT17 0EL

REV JOHN NOLAN

A young couple, just married, were at the airport awaiting a flight to their honeymoon destination. Noticing that the bridegroom appeared rather glum and distant, the bride, on inquiring the reason, was informed that this was the first Saturday in ten years that he had missed going to see his favourite football team. The bride feeling rather hurt, sarcastically suggested that he go on to the match and that they could cancel the honeymoon.

"Oh no!" replied the groom, "I wouldn't do that!"
"But why not?" said his wife icily. "If you prefer to see your team rather than go on a honeymoon don't let the honeymoon get in the way!
"Oh no!" repeated the groom, "I would not do that! - By the time I got there, the match would nearly be over!"

fisherwick church

Minister: Rev. DAVID LAPSLEY **THE PRESBYTERIAN CHURCH IN IRELAND**

Church House
4 Chlorine Gardens
BELFAST BT9 5DJ

2 April 1990

James and John were very lively twins who went to stay with their Uncle and his wife for the summer holidays. The couple had no children of their own; the Uncle was a little, hen-pecked man and his wife was a big, bossy woman who scolded him and the boys all the time.

James and John were dissatisfied with the pocket money they were receiving, so they decided to ask for more. They knew they couldn't approach their Aunt, so they cornered their Uncle on his own. "How much do you want?" he asked. "£1.00 a week each" they replied.

"A pound a week" he gasped "that's terrible."

"Do you know what I was getting when I married your Aunt?"

James thought for a moment and then replied "No! and I'll bet you didn't either."

* * * * * * * * * * * * * * * *

Dear Elizabeth

Congratulations on your excellent idea. Please find enclosed my contribution to you wedding joke book. I hope it is a great success. Perhaps I will be able to get a copy when it is published.

Yours sincerely

David Lapsley.

REV DR DAVID LAPSLEY

REV.T.H.MULLIN

24 Ratheane Avenue
COLERAINE

A TRUE ULSTER STORY

A couple were going to get married and they had just 2 witnesses the taxi driver and the sexton. The local minister did not know any of them except his own sexton.
They stood in front of the Minister who conducted the service and took their wedding vows. Then they went in to sign the register. The bride signed and then the Minister asked the man who had taken the vows to sign

"I'm just the taxi driver."

The marriage of course was not legal as they had not a proper marriage lience. Someone asked the bride afterwards how she felt when she was asked to take the taxi driver as her lawful wedded husband instead of her intended bridegroom.

She just replied "Sure they were both nice fellows!"

REV.T.H.MULLIN

24 Ratheane Avenue
COLERAINE

A coloured chap came to his employer one day and asked for a day off as his wife had died and he had to go to the funeral.
His employer gave him the day off but a few weeks afterwards he asked for another day off.

"Well John, why do you want off this time?" asked his boss.

"It's to get married" John replied.

"But sure it's only a few weeks since you buried your wife."

"Oh" said the coloured chap "that's true but I don't hold spite long."

REV J WILLIAMSON

The Bride's father had bought a Cuckoo Clock which stopped and he took it to the clock maker for repairs. When he took it home again it did go but instead of sounding "Cuckoo" at the hour it only sounded "Koo."

In a speech to the guests he declared that his daughter was not like the defaulting clock that she could "Cook" as well as "Koo."

CANON D.G.A. CLARKE

2 ASHLEY COURT
WARREN POINT
Co. DOWN BT34 3RN
TEL. 72416

2Ist.April.

Dear Lizzie,

Thank you for your letter and I wish you well with your project.

The need for patience and toleration in marriage

"The looks that over cocktails/supper look so sweet, can be so different over Shredded Wheat".

Sincerely yours,

D.G.A. Clarke.

Terrace Row Presbyterian Church

Rev. David Clarke, Ll.B., B.D.
3, Knocktarna Manor,
Coleraine,
Co. Londonderry.
BT52 IHY
(0265)55397

WE USE IT AS A FAN!

(For the purposes of this joke,use the name of an individual who ispresent at the wedding,and whose name and address are well known to others....let's say,Mr.John Smith of High Street)

A man who lived in High Street ,dreamt one evening that he had died and gone to heaven.Welcomed by St. Peter . he was taken on a guided tour of the Celestial City.

One of the first paces he was taken to, was a huge hall, where hundreds of clocks were kept on shelves all around the hall.He asked St. Peter to explain the significance of the clocks.Said St. Peter,'Each clock represents the life of each person on earth;and as the clock ticks away, so each man's life ticks away'

The newcomer to heaven noticed that here and there, there were clocks whose hands were whirling forward through 24 hours.Again he asked St.Peter to explain why this should be so."Oh, "said St.Peter.'when a man on earth kisses his wife, and tells her he loves her, he loses 24 hours of his life.That's why his clock rushes on through 24 hours.

" That's very interesting", said the newcomer."I live near Mr.John Smith in High Street.I wonder where his clock is.?"

St.Peter was perplexed."Mr.John Smith of High Street.I can't recall seeing his clock here,"he said. And then,after scratching his head for a while,St.Peter said,"John Smith of High Street? I remember now. His clock's downstairs in the kitchens.We use it as a fan!".

REV. BRIAN A. COBBE

16 Knockhill Park
BELFAST

Let me tell you about two weddings which had a funny happening in them ... they both took place in a County Donegal Church.

The first wedding that I think of had as its opening hymn "The Lord is My Shepherd," as was the custom the guests were at the front of the Church, then there were some empty pews and at the back of the Church were some friends and people who enjoyed seeing a wedding.

The organist started to play - she played a well known Tune and the people at the front of the Church sang that tune - the people at the back of the Church sang the hymn to a different Tune that of "Crimond".
A joyful send off for the couple being married!

The other wedding is one against me! The girl getting married was a very shy person - she wanted to be married quietly and no crowds of people - we arranged to marry her at 8.00 a.m. (the earliest hour for a wedding to be recognised by the state.) We set our electric alarm clock as my wife and I went to bed.
We woke in the morning - the clock showed ten to seven - we were in no hurry - at seven by our clock there was a lot of noise at our front door telling us that the Bride was in the Church. I had set the clock an hour slow! My wife was playing the organ - I was marrying the couple. I don't know how we did it but within four minutes she was at the organ and I was behind the communion rail (unshaven!) The couple were safely married with a few extra people in the Church because of the delay.

Carrickfergus Methodist Church

ALBERT ROAD/WEST STREET - CARRICKFERGUS
TELEPHONE: CARRICKFERGUS 69772

Minister:
TREVOR KENNEDY
40 LARNE ROAD
CARRICKFERGUS
Co. ANTRIM BT38 7DZ
Telephone: Carrickfergus 62202

Full-Time Assistant:
LINDA PATTERSON
2 WINDMILL AVENUE
CARRICKFERGUS
Co. ANTRIM BT38 8DH
Telephone: Carrickfergus 61886

I conducted the wedding of a young bride and groom many years ago. The bride was the most nervous bride I have ever known. To put her at ease I said to her - You don't have to worry about a thing; simply copy me. Everything I say, you say after me.

We came to the vows the bride and groom make to each other.

I said "I take you for better, for worse."
She said "I take you for better, for worse."
I said "For richer, for poorer."
She said "For richer, for poorer."
I said "In sickness and in health."
She said "In sickness and in health."
I said "Till death us do part."
She said "Till death us do part."

I was so relieved that we had got to the end of the vows without her collapsing that I said "BANG ON."

She said "BANG ON."

REVD. CANON DR. C. THORNTON, PHD., B.D., LTH.

PORTRUSH

THE FAMILY BUSINESS

Two bachelor brothers, Mick and Dick lived together on their remote farm. One day, Mick said: "I think I'll get married and bring a wife home here."
Dick: "Surely you would never do that."
Mick: "Why not?"
Dick: "Because you and I could never discuss family business in front of a stranger."

THE LAST WORD

A timid little man surprised his friend by telling him boldly:

"When my wife and I disagree, I always have the last word -

YES DEAR!"

The Presbyterian Church in Ireland

West Church, Ballymena

Clerk of Session : MR. E. F. DONAGHY, 65 Crankill Road
Secretary : MR. M. COURTNEY, 4 Dunluce Park
Treasurer : MR. S. P. TAYLOR, 47 Tullymore Park

REV. W. J. D. HENRY, B.D.
56 Cameron Park

18th March 1990.

The following are two true stories - the second one actually is something that happened to me.

a) The minister stood in front of the Bride and Groom and when he put the question to the bride - "Wilt thou have this man to be thy lawful wedded husband?"
The Brides reply was "What do you think I brought him here for?"

b) It was the first time I had ever conducted a wedding and I was terribly nervous. But as I looked up at the Groom, he was obviously even more nervous, for he was quite pale and his hands were trembling. The whole tension and anxiety of the Groom and Minister and indeed the congregation were relieved by the outburst of laughter of everybody present when the Minister asked the Groom to repeat after him - "I take this woman" - "I take this woman" "to be my lawful wedded wife" - "to be my AWFUL wedded wife!!"

The Rev. Canon Charles Howe, B.A., B.D.

St Augustine's Rectory, 4 Bridgewater, Caw,
LONDONDERRY

When I was a curate and not very experienced in taking marriage ceremonies, a bride's mother stood up to speak at the reception. She wasn't a person noted for being agreeable and I was trying to keep her on her seat and was hoping to do so. But, up she got and advised the newly-weds to take two bears with them into their new home. We shuddered; what was to follow; she didn't much approve of the groom taking away her daughter. In fact, I was to be glad that she spoke, and advised that two bears - BEAR and FORBEAR - were home essentials.

Canon J.J.G. Mercer, M.A.
Ballyholme Rectory
3 Ward Avenue
Bangor, Co. Down
BT20 5JW
Telephone: Bangor 454836

I like the little story about the Church of Ireland Rector who instructed a rather nervous bridegroom not to forget the responses in the marriage service. Unfortunately the poor man managed to get his lines mixed up that when the Rector came to the point in the service where he said -

"I pronounce that they be man and wife together," the bridegroom responded loud and clear -

"LORD, HAVE MERCY UPON US."

Stormont Presbyterian Church

618 Upper Newtownards Road, Belfast BT4 3HA Phone 656637

Minister
Rev. Dr. J. Ronald Savage
1 Knockdarragh Park
Belmont Road
Belfast BT4 2LE
Phone 768155

Clerk of Session
Dr. John Patton
7 Knockdarragh Park
Belmont Road
Belfast BT4 2LE
Phone 63401

Secretary
Mr. Jim Irvine
25 Kensington Road
Knock
Belfast BT5 6NH
Phone 794279

Treasurer
Mr. Colin Boyd
43 Knocklofty Park
Belfast BT4 3NB
Phone 671605

Did you hear about the bride's father who broke his false teeth during the meal at the wedding reception. Already very nervous this put him in a real panic about his speech. He went to the mens room to see if he could effect an emergency repair on the dentures. While he was doing this another man observed his problem and asked if he could help: He had a a spare pair of teeth. The Bride's father tried them but they were far too small. "Don't worry I have another set" said the man and produced a second set from a pocket. Alas these were far too large. Panic set in again. "Try these ones" said the man producing yet another set of teeth from another pocket. These ones fitted perfectly "Am I not, the lucky man" said the bride's father, "to have met a dentist when I was in this predicament". "Oh I'm not a dentist" said the man "I'm an undertaker".

Rev. J. Herman Brown

'Escalo'
6 Cambourne Park
Finvoy Road
Ballymoney
BT53 7PG
Tel: 65738

I3/2/'90

MISS SHONA KIRK,
COLERAINE.

DEAR SHONA,

I'm very sorry for being so la in replying......indeed, maybe I'm too late....

But here goes....

Two nuns in a Mini Metro were going shopping, The One said to the other . I'm going into the Super-market, and you can take the car round the block and when you come back I'll be waiting for you with the messages.

'Right', said the other, 'I'll do that.'

But when the nun came out of the Super-market, she couldn't see any sign of her friend. So she said to a man who hapened to be passing by, 'By the way , have you seen a nun in a red mini?'.

He answered, 'No, but I would like to..!'.

Just for good measure, here's another.

Three clergymen, a presbyterian, a Church of Ireland and a Methodi were travelling together in the South of England, and unfortunatel each of the ministers was a little deaf and this was aggrava te by the clatter of the wheels of the train in which they were travelling together.
As the train stopped at a station, the Presbyterian said, 'I say, is this Wembly?'.
To which the Church of Ireland clergy replied'No, I think it's Thursday.'
And the methodist added'So am I, let's go for a Coke!'.

O.K. Shona, I hope you'll like one of them!

All good wishes,

Yours,

J.H.B.

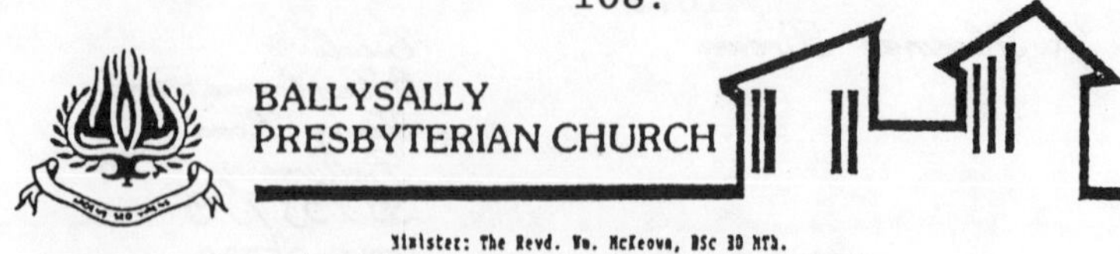

Minister: The Revd. Wm. McKeown, BSc BD MTh.
2 Cloonavin Park, Coleraine, N. Ireland BT52 1BU Tel 0265 53336

27 Jan 1990

Rev. Wm. McKeown, BSc, BD, MTh.

TRUE STORY

This is a true story told to me by the caretaker of a church. He had opened the church for the wedding, the groom etc had arrived. The bride called in on the way home from the hairdresser and asked the caretaker if the groom had arrived. He told her that he had.

She then said "In that case I will go home and get changed." Clearly she had little confidence in her husband to be!

"KINGSTON"
23 Kilraughts Road,
BALLYMONEY,
G. E. Lockhart *Co. Antrim BT53 7AL.*

A wife not long married gave her husband his evening meal. As he was eating it, the wife said "I am very good at making apple tart and steak and kidney pie". The husband looked up from what he was eating and asked "Tell me dear is that apple tart or is it steak and kidney pie?"

A girl was getting married. She had very little money and could not afford the money to buy the sugar to ice her wedding cake. A friend of hers was recently married. She asked her "did you put icing on your wedding cake?" "Oh no" was the reply "I just white washed mine".

The Salvation Army was conducting an open air meeting. The time came for the collection. One of the collectors went to the Captain and said "that lovely girl over there put £5 in the box". The Captain said "go and ask her if there is a hymn she would like?" The member of the Army went to her and asked. "Is there any hymn you would like?" "Oh yes" she said "I would like him that beats the big drum".

"KINGSTON"
23 Kilraughts Road,
BALLYMONEY,
G. E. Lockhart *Co. Antrim BT53 7AD.*

A woman who was middle-aged was not married. She was worried about her position, Christmas was coming and she thought of the children hanging up their stockings. She decided to write to Santa Claus, in the letter she wrote "Dear Santa Claus help me if you can I have hung up a pair of trousers please shove in a man".

A couple returned from their honeymoon. The young wife made a terrible mistake for her husband's breakfast she gave him soap flakes instead of cornflakes. She told a friend about it. The friend asked was he mad. "Mad" said the wife "he was foaming at the mouth".

Two women were waiting for a bus in Belfast. A double decker came along. The conductor said "one up and one down". One of the women said "surely you would not separate a daughter from her mother?" The conductor said "I did that once in my life and I will not do it again".

A man and his wife were married for 50 years. Someone asked the husband "did you have any secrets which you kept from one another?" "Oh yes" said the husband "I have £5000 in the bank that the wife knows nothing about and the wife has £1000 that I know nothing about".

"KINGSTON"
23 Kilraughts Road,
BALLYMONEY,
G. E. Lockhart Co. Antrim BT53 7AD.

A young man went for a walk with his girl friend. He said to her "Last night I dreamt I proposed to you. What does it mean?" The girl said "I think that it means that you have more sense when you are asleep than when you are awake".

A young couple recently married. The husband said to his wife, "there is one thing about you, you cannot make cakes like my mother", to which the wife replied "there is one thing about you, you cannot make dough like my father".

BALTEAGH and BOVEVAGH PRESBYTERIAN CHURCHES

Minister: Rev. James Clarke, B.A.

Telephone:
Limavady 62474.

Balteagh Manse,
30 Ballyleagry Road,
LIMAVADY,
Co. Londonderry,
BT49 0NJ.

2nd February 90.

Dear Shona,

Thank you for your letter and photograph. What a lovely girl you are, I expect you will soon be getting married. Find below a few things that I say at Weddings.

There was a Lady who had the habit of getting married and divorced a short time later. She married in turn a Millionaire,an Actor, a Clergyman and an Undertaker......
"One for the money, Two for the Show, Three to get ready and Four to Go."

A Game Keepers advice to newly Weds. "May the Deer season never end and the Grouse season never begin."

ANONYMOUS

A couple were getting married late in life and for some reason there was no chance to have a rehearsal before the ceremony. All went well until just after the rings were exchanged.

The couple were told by the Minister in a whisper: "Will you both please kneel down at the rail."
The ageing bride whispered back a little louder "Well, I could get down alright but I may never get up!"

You see? this is the best I can do. It would have to be ANONYMOUS because it actually happened and if my name was connected with it the names of the people concerned could be leaked out!

Dunluce Presbyterian Church

Minister—
REV. JOHN HUME, B.A.
21 PRIESTLAND ROAD
BUSHMILLS BT57 8XB
Tel. 31358

Clerk of Session
ROBERT A. McILROY
174a STRAID ROAD
BUSHMILLS BT57 8XW
Tel 31629

Church Secretary—I. BINNIE, B.A., 8 MARINE DRIVE, PORTBALLINTRAE, BUSHMILLS BT57 8RP

An Irishman was visiting Paris for the first time. Out for a walk he saw a crowd of people gathered at a Church door. Curious he joined the crowd and was just in time to see bride and groom emerge after their wedding.

"Who's getting married?" he asked a nearby spectator.
The spectator replied:- "Je ne sais pas."
"Thanks" said the Irishman.

A couple of days later he came on a group of people watching a funeral pass by.

"Who's dead?" he asked a man beside.
The man replied:- "Je ne sais pas."

"Heth" said the Irishman, "He didn't last long!"

REV H HOPKINS

The Rectory
10 Coleraine Road
Portrush
Co Antrim

Jones came home one evening and found his young wife sobbing.

"What's the matter, darling?" he asked anxiously.
Amidst the sobs, she explained that the cat had eaten all the cakes she had made that morning.

"Never mind, old dear," he said kindly, I'll get you another cat tomorrow."

"I can see you are a married man, now."

"How?"

"Cause you have no buttons off your coat and-"

"Yes, that's the first thing my wife did - taught me how to sew them on."

Belfast Central Mission
Grosvenor Hall
5 Glengall Street
Belfast
BT12 5AD
Telephone Belfast 241917

Superintendent:
Rev. DAVID J. KERR, B.A.

CENTRES OF WORK:
Grosvenor Hall, Belfast

Craigmore Adolescent Home, Millisle, Co. Down

Childhaven Conference Centre and Holiday Home, Millisle, Co. Down

Castle Rocklands House and Bungalows for Senior Citizens, Carrickfergus, Co. Antrim

14 March 1990

Miss Jillian Boyd
13 Cairnmount Park
Coleraine
Co Londonderry.

Dear Jillian,

Thank you for your letter asking for a funny wedding story or joke. I thought it was a nice idea to include a photograph of yourself as it helps me to see the nice person who has this name, Jillian Boyd.

I have been scratching my head and trying to think of a story or joke that you might be able to use, and it is very hard to find one which is still funny when it is written down. However, I hope the following might be useful to you and your friends.

"Jim had three girls that he liked very much but couldn't make up his mind which one he wanted to take out, so he asked the advice of his friend, Tom. Tom wanted to know something about the girls so Jim explained that Mary was a barmaid, Ann was a telephonist and Gillian was a school teacher. Tom replied that he thought he should go out with Gillian, the school teacher. The reason he gave was as follows, when you take Mary home and are kissing her good night she will say 'Time, gentlemen, please', when you are taking Ann home and kissing her good night, she will say, 'Your three minutes are up', but when you are taking Gillian home and you are kissing her good night, she will say, 'I am not satisfied with that, we will have to do it again'.

I hope your book of wedding humour will be a great success and that you will be able to make a good contribution to the restoration fund in your church.

Yours sincerely,

David J Kerr

David J Kerr.

Carlisle Road Presbyterian Church

LONDONDERRY

Minister: THE REV. RICHARD C. GRAHAM, B.A., 59 Limavady Road.
Telephone: Londonderry 42478

27th April 1990

"Why is marriage like a beseiged city?"

"Those outside want in and those inside want out."

REV STEPHEN D HAZLETT, CURATE.

HOLY TRINITY CHURCH PORTRUSH

The best I can think of is that some years ago in Co Cavan a rather nervous bridegroom stood up at the Reception to record his appreciations and blubbered out

"I want to thank you all from the bottom of my heart ... and from my wife's bottom also!"

The Methodist Church in Ireland

Londonderry Mission Circuit

Superintendent Minister
Rev. Kenneth Best

11, Clearwater
Clooney Rd.
Londonderry

27. 2. 90

The Minister was talking to the couple before their wedding. He wanted to know did the groom know anything about marriage. He asked the groom to give him a quotation from the Bible that proved a man was only allowed one wife at a time. The young man thought for a while and gave his answer,

"NO MAN CAN SERVE TWO MASTERS!!"

The newly wed man had looked forward all day to having Rhubarb pie for his dessert. When he came home his wife told him she hadn't any. When he asked why, she told him she had searched the whole town for a Rhubarb pie dish BUT COULDN'T FIND ONE LONG ENOUGH!!

SUBJECT REF.

DATE Jan.23/90

14 Craigaboney Road, Bushmills, Co. Antrim. BT57 8XD Telephone: 31180

Shona Kirk
3 Cairnvale
Coleraine

Dear Shona,

I received your letter and wish you every success in your project. Hope my little contribution can be of some use to you.

The wedding I refer to was not being conducted by myself but a fellow minister in Belfast. As you can appreciate weddings are the sort of things that everyone wants to run smoothly and without any problems. My associate Mr. Stevenson was waiting by the altar for the bride to march up the aisle with her father. It was [illegible] prior to the entrance being made when one of the guests on the bridegrooms side had been in the minister's room. Hearing the procession commencing and not wishing to emerge out of the minister's room causing a distraction she decided to tip toe across the baptistery and exit by a side door into her seat. Since baptism in this church is by immersion you will appreciate that the baptistery is quite large and containing a lot of water.
The lady, not being a member of this church was unaware of this. She tip toed across the plastic covering of the baptistery and SPLASH. She was under. I mean everything, UNDER. The splash and the scream created such a distraction that the procession had to be delayed while the matter was investigated. She was helped out of the water dripping wet and so ashamed. I think if she had the choice she'd rather have drowned.
A wedding and a baptism on the one day.
(Between you and me, I think our Lord would have laughed at this one.)

Let me know when your book is ready Shona and I shall be happy to purchase a copy.

Love and best wishes,

R.J.Ritchie
Minister
Artillery Rd. Church of Christ.

BAPTISTERY.

REV.F.A.ROBINSON

BALLYMONEY

This minister announced where and when he would be visiting during the week. This gave the people an idea when to expect him.

He came to a certain farm house and to his knocking, the door was opened by the daughter called Mary.

"Mary is your mother in?" the minister asked.

"No" said Mary "she went to town on the 10 o'clock bus!"

"And what bus did she say she would be coming back on?" the minister asked.

Mary stepped back a little "mother" she called "what bus did you say I was to tell him you were coming back on?"

THE METHODIST CHURCH IN IRELAND

Donegal & Ballintra Circuit

Superintendent Minister:

METHODIST MANSE,
LAGHEY,
CO. DONEGAL,
REPUBLIC OF IRELAND

Telephone: 073-21825
(0018- from N.I.)

14 March 1990

Miss Jillian Boyd
13 Cairnmount Park
Coleraine
N Ireland
BT5 3JR

Dear Jillian

What a good idea you have had to raise money for your Church. Here is my best wedding joke.

There was a Donegal farmer who had a sheep who kept banging his head against a wall. He called the vet and he suggested that the farmer play music to the sheep, and he assured him this would work, he had seen this happen before.

The farmer brought out the old gramophone and did what the vet said and when he went out the next morning, he found the sheep was dead.

He called the vet, who was very surprised and he asked the farmer, what music did you play? The farmer replied, my only record by Frank Sinatra, the hit record "I'll never find another You" (ewe)

Good luck with your book and the restoration of your Church. Enclosed is your envelope, we cannot use it from the Republic.

Yours sincerely,

Rev B Griffin

Portrush,

Dear Elizabeth,

Thankyou for your letter requesting a best or funniest wedding story. I am sorry for not replying sooner, but I overlooked your request. The following little story is quite humorous, but often it is the manner in which stories are told that makes them more enjoyable.

A father and his son were sitting talking beside the open fire. In a few days the son would be getting married. The younger man became very quiet and thoughtful as the evening passed.

" Is there anything troubling you?" asked the father. " Well"said the son " It's the thought of getting married. It's a big step leaving home, and especially when it involves starting out in life with a strange woman."

" Don't be worrying son " said the old man " everything will be O.K. I also thought like you, but found there was no need for concern"

The son looked at him and replied"But it was all right for you da, sure you married my ma."

You can just make this an anonymous story as I heard it from someone else. I would like to purchase a copy of your book " Wedding Humour " when it is produced.

Yours sincerely

THE IRISH MISSION
Room 209
Church House
Belfast
N. Ireland

Dear Elizabeth,

Thank you for your letter requesting a wedding story. I do not have a great lot of these so I hope the following may be of help:

[1] A Scottish gentleman was on holiday in London when he got into conversation with an Englishman. The Englishman enquired about the purpose of his visit to London, thinking that perhaps he was on a business trip. He was somehwat surprised when the Scottish gentleman stated that he was on his honeymoon. When asked where his new wife was, the Scot replied,"There was no sense in bringing her along as she had already been to London."

[2] Marriage requires a man to exercise the virtue of diplomacy. Someone once described a diplomat as the man who was able to persuade his wife that woman looked fat in fur coats!

[3] Did you hear about the Ballymena wife who was expecting her fifth baby. Her husband came home and found her in tears. Asking what was the matter, she pointed to the headlines in the local newspaper which stated,"Every fifth baby born in world is Chinese"!

I am also returning your photo so that you can use it again,

Yours sincerely,

David J. Temple

THE METHODIST CHURCH IN IRELAND

CLONTARF, SUTTON and SKERRIES CIRCUIT

THE MANSE,
CHURCH ROAD,
SUTTON,
DUBLIN 13

REV. KENNETH H. THOMPSON, M.A.
Tel. 323143

22 March 1990

Dear Shona

I'm not very good at remembering jokes and most of the ones that I tell at wedding receptions are personal and about the people concerned, e.g. My wife and I were married in a little Presbyterian Church in a border village in Co. Armagh. We waited, and waited, for my minister to arrive from Dublin but had to start without him. As we were finishing the first hymn we saw him rushing past the side of the church and in a couple of minutes he came out of the vestry looking very breathless.

Afterwards he told us that he and the friends who were travelling with him had delayed too long over a cup of coffee on the journey. When he reached the village he asked where the church was the

Continued overleaf .....

policeman on duty said, "It's down there, and you'd better hurry. You're in the North now and things start on time up here!" [That minister was actually a Belfast man - I had better keep his name a secret!!].

Here are a few short jokes about married couples -

Husband:"Are you ready, dear?"
Wife: "Be quiet! I've been telling you for the last hour I'll be ready in a minute."

Marie Corelli, the novelist, was asked why she had never got married.
"I don't need a husband. I've got a dog that growls all morning, a parrot that swears all afternoon, and a cat that stays out all night".

Yours sincerely

Ken Thompson (Rev.)

The Methodist Church in Ireland

Secretary of the Conference:
Rev. Charles G. Eyre, B.A.
1 Fountainville Avenue
Belfast BT9 6AN
Tel. (0232) 224554

5 April 1990.

Dear Jillian,

I was at a meeting last week and the Archbishop of Canterbury told us this story. I hope you think it is funny enough for your book.

With very best wishes,
Yours most sincerely,

Charles G. Eyre

Rev. Charles G. Eyre.

A Jewish Rabbi and a Roman Catholic Bishop were sitting side by side at a dinner. There was a choice of two items on the Menu, Quiche and Pork Stew. The R.C. Bishop chose Pork Stew and when the Rabbi asked for Quiche the Bishop said to him:
"Why not try the Pork Stew? it is delicious"
But the Rabbi still asked for the Quiche.
When the meals arrived the Bishop turned to the Rabbi and said "You should have had this Pork Stew, it looks very good."
But the Rabbi still took his Quiche.
After a few minutes the Bishop turned to the Rabbi again and said to him "You really snould have had this Pork Stew; it is excellent".
To which the Rabbi replied "Does your wife often make you Pork Stew at home?"
The Bishop then told the Rabbi that R.C. Bishops do not have wives to which the Rabbi replied: "Well, I think I would rather have my wife than Pork Stew!"

The Methodist Church in Ireland
Castlederg Circuit

REV DENIS ANDERSON

There is a true story about a wedding in a Presbyterian church near here, many years ago. The Minister was new to the area, and did not know the people. He met the groom and best man in the vestry. He said to the bestman "Are you the groom?" The bestman thought he said, "Are you Muldoon?" and he answered "Yes". So, it is said, the Minister married the bestman to the bride and was not told about this till after the service! I can't imagine how the people went through with the wedding without telling the Minister his mistake - but that's the story I was told.

A similar story concerns a Church of England Minister in the last century. Easter Day was popular for weddings and several couples would be married at once. The Minister read through the marriage service only once, for everybody. One Easter, the couples got a little mixed and the Minister shouted out, "Sort yourselves when you get out!"

REV CANON DR.C. THORNTON, PH.D., B.D.,LTH.
PORTRUSH

A ROOM WITH NO VIEW

A Bride and groom were on honeymoon in a 25 storeyed hotel. The groom went for a walk inside the vast building, and forgot the number of his room. He tramped up floors and down and knocked on dozens of doors, calling out, - "Honey! is that you?" - but no luck. Exhausted, he at last knocked on one more door, and desperately called out - "Honey! Honey! let me in." No answer. Again he called, "Honey! it's me." The door opened about 6 inches and a bearded face appeared; then a voice rasped - "I don't know what your game is, but this is a W.C., not a Beehive."

THE SECOND CHANCE TO ESCAPE

Not like today's Bride, this lady was no beauty. Indeed the clergyman must have felt sorry for the groom, but proceeded with the service -
Clergyman: "Will you have this woman to be your wife?"
Groom: "I will."
Clergyman: "NOW, I'LL ASK YOU AGAIN!"

REV. VICTOR HANSON

KILLOWEN PARISH CHURCH COLERAINE

STORY

During a wedding service the bride was put in a very embarrassing situation. At the point in the service when I asked the best man for the ring he began furiously to search his pockets, eventually he found the ring, but on it being placed by the bridegroom on his bride's finger she looked at the bridegroom with scorn and said - "This is not the ring - it's too big
- this is your ring - the one I bought you."
Again the best man began searching his pockets and finally produced the right ring, so the service ended joyfully, but just how the day ended for the best man I've yet to learn?

JOKES

Clergyman called in a repair man to get his television working again. The job completed, the Minister ever mindful of the pennies, said "Remember, I'm only a poor preacher of the Gospel.
"I know", said the repair man, "I've heard you."

REV. VICTOR HANSON

KILLOWEN PARISH CHURCH COLERAINE

A Jew on his deathbed, called his wife Becca to his bedside and said to her, " Becca, you stood by me when I came home wounded.
You stood by me when my business failed.
And now you're standing by me as I die.
Becca - You've been the Jinx of my life."

Mrs Malone was at her wits end over her husbands drinking, and finally turned to her Minister for advice. "What he needs is a good fright", said the Minister "this is what you must do. Wait for him by the cemetery tonight, wrap yourself in a white sheet and jump at him when he passes."

And so late that night, Mrs Malone went down to the graveyard, draped herself in the sheet and waited.
It wasn't long before her husband lurched into view. As he drew level, she sprang out in front of him and cried, "I'm the devil."
The husband looked at the apparition. Then he stretched out his hand slurred,
"Put it there, friend. I'm married to your sister!"

Trinity Presbyterian Church

Minister: Rev. Dr. R.E.H. UPRICHARD, B.A. B.D., M.Th.
Trinity Manse, Ahoghill, Co. Antrim, N. Ireland BT42 1JU
Telephone: Ahoghill 871270

Clerk of Session: W. Dickey, J.P.
55 Oldpark Rd., Ballymena, Tel. 656957

A teacher gave pupils words to place in sentences for homework to show that they understood the meaning. A little girl was given the word FASCINATE.

The minister called that night at her home. Next day she brought the following sentence to school.

Last night the minister called at our house and had his tea. When he arrived he had nine buttons on his coat. When he left he could only FASCINATE.

VERY REV H. LECKEY

The Abbey Rectory
5 Downshire Road
BANGOR
Co Down

The rather elderly bride was partially deaf and was concerned about making her vows during the wedding ceremony.

"Don't worry," the rector reassured her, "when the time comes, I will give you a nod and you then make your vows."

Unfortunately the poor lady opened her Prayer Book at the Confirmation Service instead of the Service of Holy Matrimony and when the rector, having posed the question -

"Wilt thou have this man as thy wedded husband?", nodded to her, she drew herself up to her full height and in a loud voice shouted out -

"I RENOUNCE THE DEVIL!"

Enclosed is a little golfing story which my be of some use to you, but do not put my name to it. All success with your fund raising venture.

GOLFING STORY

Two men went golfing every Monday. Nothing (rain, hail, snow) was allowed to interfere with this activity. Then one day, as a funeral passed along the road beside the golf course, one of the men left down his golf club, took off his cap and stood to attention as the hearse passed.

His companion was surprised and said "I've never before seen you let anything interfere with your game of golf." "True", said his friend, "but the person they are laying to rest to-day has been my wife for the best part of 40 years!"

From: The Rev. Dr. I.M. Ellis

TEL: TANDRAGEE 840221

(S.T.D. Code 0762
R.o.I. Code 08-0762)

THE RECTORY
89 MULLAVILLY ROAD
TANDRAGEE
CO. ARMAGH BT62 2LX
NORTHERN IRELAND

25th April 1990

Dear Jillian,

Thank you for your letter requesting my favourite wedding story for inclusion in your proposed book in aid of your church restoration fund. This is a great idea - so here goes!

> A best man had been in trouble with the Law. In fact, he had been up before the magistrates on quite a few occasions. To the amazement of the officiating rector who did not know this man's background, when it came to the point in the marriage service when he was to place the ring on the Prayer Book, he instead placed his hand on it and said, "I swear to tell the truth, the whole truth, and nothing but the truth"!

I hope you find this story amusing too. Please let me know when your book is published. I'd like to order a copy right away.

With best wishes,
Yours sincerely,

Ian M. Ellis

3, S.John's Close,
Portstewart.
22nd Jan., 1990.

Dear Jillian,

Thank you for your letter asking for some funny story for the book "Wedding Humour" to which you want to contribute for your Church Restoration Fund.

As I am some years retired I can't remember many such but perhaps the following two may help, both relating to a very nervous bride-to-be.

Minister at Service : Wilt thou have this man to be thy wedded husband.....?
Bride: I wilt.

Later at Reception one of her friends who knew how nervous she was sent the following telegram : "Cheer up; 1 John 4, 18" which reads: 'There is no fear in love; but perfect love casteth out fear' However the Post Office misquoted the reference and the Best Man read the telegram thus: "Cheer up John 4, 18" and then found the passage and read - 'Thou hast had 5 husbands and he whom thou now hast is not thine husband'.

However Jillian I hope you yourself read the Bible daily and will love it and trust in your Saviour so that you will be able to quote it accurately and to give an answer to anyone who asks you why you believe it - cp 1 Peter 3. 15.

God bless you now and always

Cecil A. B. Williams

Bill Nesbitt

THE WEDDING SPEECH

Unaccustomed, as I am, to public speaking,
I am standing here before you all today
All because my little daughter
Did some things she didn't oughter ...
And I'm not exactly pleased, I have to say ...

Now, first of all, there's something I must tell you,
Something that I feel you ought to know -
Because of all their messing,
They haven't got my blessing,
And their marriage, I admit, has been a blow ...

But, anyway, they've been and gone and done it,
And so we're gathered here at this reception -
And I've little sense of pride
When I see the blushing bride,
For she's blushing at the thought of her deception ...

It's only very recently I met him,
This husband that she's taken on for life -
And, from all I've heard about him,
She'd be better off without him,
For she could have been some wealthy banker's wife ...

We brought her up in decency and virtue,
And trained her to be honest, good and fair -
But everything we'd taught her
Was forgotten by my daughter
When she met that grinning idiot, over there!

I've always had a certain reputation
As someone who will call a spade a spade -
So there's no point in pretending
That we'll see a happy ending,
For, together, they've no future, I'm afraid ...

Bill Nesbitt

THE WEDDING SPEECH (Cont'd.)

His parents, now, I think I ought to mention,
And both of them, for coming, I must thank -
Their very generous gift
Showed a proper sense of thrift ...
And it didn't do much damage in their bank ...

I'm glad to see his family all assembled,
His friends, and his relations, by the score -
Their meals have been demolished
And their plates are clean and polished
As they sit there hoping, maybe, there'll be more ...

I don't intend to bore you lot much longer,
For you're not the sort of company I'd choose -
You haven't time for speeches,
For you're sitting there, like leeches,
Hoping that I'll soon break out the booze ...

Well, now our families both are joined together,
United at this happy wedding feast,
Our hearts and spirits blending
At this fairy story ending ...
The fairy tale of Beauty ... and the Beast ...!

Oh, nurse - I wonder ... may I ask a favour?
This bandage is too tight around my head ...
It doesn't make much sense
Why those people took offence ...
I wonder ... was it something that I said ...?

GREAT VICTORIA STREET
BAPTIST CHURCH
BELFAST, BT2 7BB

Pastor: Trevor C. Brock, 27 Eastleigh Drive, Upper Newtownards Road, Belfast BT4 3DX. *Tel. 657880.*
Secretary: Martin McMichael, 9 Lenaghan Avenue, Belfast BT8 4JF. *Tel. Belfast 702258*
Treasurer: J. Harold Stewart, 34 Beechgrove Avenue BT6 ONF. *Tel. Belfast 795699*

138.

20.3.90.

The missionary in India conducted a traditional Christian Wedding, and afterwards a Hindu told the missionary he had really enjoyed the Christian Wedding. He asked if the missionary would conduct a wedding for him.

On the arranged date, the missionary arrived at the church, and was shocked to find that the Indian gentleman had 16 wives!

The missionary told him there must be a misunderstanding.

"No!" He replied, "I heard you say, 4 better, 4 worse, 4 richer, and 4 poorer!"

From the Revd. Derek J. McKelvey,

Ballygilbert Presbyterian Church,

Co. Down

There was a bachelor of about 35 who had been going steady for a couple of years when he won £2,500 on a Premium Bond. Although he was very pleased at his good fortune it gave him a bit of a problem as he couldn't decide wnether to get married with the money or to have a garage built for his car.

So he asked his neighbour's advice - but the neighbour said that on such a matter he could not help the bachelor make up his mind.
The neighbour didn't see the fellow for a few weeks but one day a lorry-load of bricks arrived and the neighbour being curious went round to see the bachelor.

"Well" said the neighbour "I see that you decided on the garage"

"Yes" said the bachelor "I decided that I could back out of it!"

FIRST COLERAINE PRESBYTERIAN CHURCH

REV DAVID MCILWRATH

"How did the wedding go today?", the Caretaker asked the Organist.

"Not too well, I'm afraid," replied the Organist. "The Minister's squint got him into trouble again."

"Oh no!" exclaimed the Caretaker, "What did he do this time?"

"He married the groom to the best man, kissed the register, and locked the bride in the Church safe!"

REV.J.ROONEY

Cloughfern Rectory
126 Doagh Road
NEWTOWNABBEY

SAYING

"Mother-in-laws are like EXORCET Missiles, no matter how you manoeuvre they score a direct hit."

The Methodist Church in Ireland
Castlederg Circuit

REV DENIS ANDERSON

Two small things which have happened to me, but which were not so funny at the time, were-

The bride's mother arriving at church to find she had left her hat at home. She had to go all the way back and the wedding was delayed by half an hour.

On another occasion, I was at the back of a church with the bride and her father, ready to walk up the aisle. But we couldn't get the organist to stop playing what she was playing, and start to play the Bridal March. It was some minutes before she realised that we were all waiting for her!

REV JOHN BEAMISH

62, FARLOUGH LANE
NEWMILLS
DUNGANNON

TRUE STORIES

The bride lived at the end of a long lane. On the morning of her wedding some miscreant cut down a tree that cut off her home from the main road, there was the customary lateness for the wedding. Then about a hour and a half later the blockage which was two hundred yards from her home was encountered. When she got to the church the organist had gone but the choir members were there. We sang an extra hymn and after all the excitement everything went well.

Another Wedding

I thought there was a certain uneasiness on the part of the groom. So I went down to the door with the newly weds. Arriving just in time to see a large car hauling a cattle trailer in through the church gates. Four young men got out, laid hands on the groom and took him off to a pub.

They returned about 2 hours later, with the groom aloft. All very drunk throughout the reception and were in a most uncomfortable state - having to make constant journeys to the toilets.

REV STOKES

THE CATHEDRAL CHURCH OF ST. MACHAR

GOOD ADVICE TO A GROOM on his wedding day, "always make sure you have the final say if you have an argument with your wife, two wee words

YES DEAR!"

7th COLERAINE GIRL GUIDE COMPANY

WEDDING STORIES

John and Mary where down from Belfast on their honeymoon in Portstewart.

Upon their first night they strolled along the beach in the moonlight and sat there romantically gazing out over the water. Presently John quoted: "Roll on thou dark and deep blue ocean, roll!" Whereupon the young bride grasped her husband's arm and exclaimed: "Oh John, dear, look - how wonderful you are - it's doing it."

THE PARISH CHURCH HILLSBOROUGH CO DOWN

REV JOHN DINNEN

A man jumped from a plane only to find his parachute would not open. On the way downwards he passed someone going upwards. He shouted "Do you know anything about parachutes?"

"No, do you know anything about gas cookers?", came the reply.

Three ministers, a Methodist, Anglican, and Presbyterian were discussing what they did with the offering.
One said "I take all the coins and give God the notes."
Another said "I make a line down the middle and one half is for God and one for me."
Third said (no names!) "I throw it all up in the air and say God, whatever you want you keep and what comes down, I keep."

Rev D.C. Searle

BANGOR

Two men engaged in the tayloring business had fallen on hard times. One Jack, said to his colleague, Glenn, "I'm leaving this old back street shop. Come with me and we'll start a new business." But Glenn, being more cautious, was reluctant, "I'll stay on here. You seek your fortune", he said to Jack. So Jack left.

Six months later, Jack paid a visit to his old friend Glenn still working away in the dingy back street premises. To Glenn's amazement, Jack was clearly rolling in money: a chauffeur driven Rolls Royce, a suit from Saville Row, a gold watch and chain.

Jack explained "I went into the meat trade. But nowadays, you have to specialise. So I thought of a new line - Chicken sausages."

"I wouldn't have thought there was as much money as that in chicken sausages," gasped Glenn, "What's your secret?"
Jack lowered his voice and spoke confidentially, "Actually," he said, "the profit isn't in the chicken meat, it's in horse flesh. You see, I add a little horse flesh to my sausages - and that's where the money is." Glenn contemplated for a moment, then asked, "Tell me, what proportion of horse flesh to chicken meat?" Jack answered, "I've always been a man of principle. I make it strictly 50 - 50 - 1 horse to 1 chicken."

LADIES AND GENTLEMEN - MARRIAGE CAN ONLY WORK IF THERE IS GIVE AND TAKE 50 - 50. But it has to be a genuine 50 - 50 not 1 horse, 1 chicken, etc etc.

Coleraine Congregational Church

NEW ROW - COLERAINE

Secretary:
MR. WILLIAM MITCHELL
30A Rosemary Place
Coleraine BT52 2AU
Telephone: 3956

Minister:
REV. COLIN McFARLAND
22 Portstewart Road
Coleraine BT52 1RN
Telephone: 2370

Treasurer:
MR. GEORGE NIXON
3 Ballycranny Drive
Coleraine BT51 3JX
Telephone: 3676

REV.COLIN McFARLAND

Not long after a young couple were married, things were not working out so well; so they sent for the Minister. After listening to their complaints he finally said;
"Bill, whenever she burns the dinner, don't you lose your temper, just go out to the front garden and cool off." Turning to the young woman, he said;
"and Maggie, when he comes in late, and you feel like hitting him with the rolling pin, just you go out to the back garden and cool off."

Now the story goes that this couple lived to a ripe old age - because they were always out in the fresh air.

Coleraine Congregational Church

NEW ROW - COLERAINE

Secretary:
MR. WILLIAM MITCHELL
30A Rosemary Place
Coleraine BT52 2AU
Telephone: 3956

Minister:
REV. COLIN McFARLAND
22 Portstewart Road
Coleraine BT52 1RN
Telephone: 2370

Treasurer:
MR. GEORGE NIXON
3 Ballycranny Drive
Coleraine BT51 3JX
Telephone: 3676

From Church Magazine

A GOOD WEDDING CAKE

4 lb of love
I lb butter of youth
½ lb of good looks
I lb of sweet temper
I lb of blindness to faults
I lb of self-forgetfulness
I lb of pounded wit
I lb of good humour
2 tablespoons of sweet argument
I pint of rippling laughter
I glass of common sense
I oz of modesty

Put the love, good looks and sweet temper into a well-furnished house. Beat the butter of youth to a cream and mix well together with the blindness to faults. Stir the pounded wit and good humour into the sweet argument, then add the rippling laughter and common sense. Work the whole together until everything is well mixed and bake gently forever.

Ballywillan Presbyterian Church

Portrush, Co. Antrim.

Minister: Rev. James Frazer,

Ballywillan Manse, 95 Gateside Road, Portrush BT56 8NP

"Marriage is like playing cards.
You start off with holding a hand,
and end up with a full house."

A man married a very ugly girl, and they went to London for their honeymoon. There they made the usual tours and visited the waxworks of Madam T.

They were going through, looking at all the wax figures and reached the Chamber of Horrors, when one of the officials came up to them. Pointing to the bride, he asked the man "Is she with You?" "If she is, would you tell her to keep moving, for we are doing stock-taking, and that's the third time we have counted her!"

REV. ROBIN LAVERY

ST. PATRICK'S RECTORY BALLYMONEY

A grandfather was discussing the Bible with his grandson.
"Were you in the ark?" asked the grandson.
"No", laughed grandfather.
"Then why weren't you drowned?"

To tell the truth I have a sneaking admiration for Noah, for he had the initiation to float his company when the rest of the world was in liquidation.

The family hamster died. Christopher, its five year-old owner, wished to give it a decent burial in the garden. He rallied his young friends and conducted a service. From the kitchen window his mother heard him despatch the hamster: "In the name of the Father, and of the Son, and into the hole he goes."

Kindly donated by Mr Willie Lake

157 Bushmills Road
COLERAINE

Little Bobby was sitting with his mother in Church during the Wedding of her eldest daughter. Halfway through the service, he observed his mother crying.

"Why are you crying Mama?" he asked, "It's not your Wedding."

When the late Mr and Mrs Henry Ford celebrated their Golden Wedding anniversary a reporter asked them
"To what do you attribute your fifty years of successful married life?"
"The formula" said Ford, "is the same formula I have always used in making cars - just stick to one model."

James proposing to Sarah! - "How would you like to bury along with our folk?"

Rev Fleming

During a television interview, a Minister was asked what was the best piece of advice he had ever been given.

He said that it was to marry the girl who was now his wife.

He was then pressed to say who had given him this good advice, to which he replied "She did."

Rev Roy Lester

Macosquin, Coleraine.

A man heard his wife referred to one day as a 'Model Wife.' Not sure what this meant he went home and took down the dictionary. He read out the following ....

"A NON-WORKING MINIATURE OF THE REAL THING!"

REV DERMOT MCMORRAN BANGOR

MINISTER of TRINITY PRESBYTERIAN CHURCH

Some years ago, when I was minister in a Belfast Congregation, I was present at a wedding reception. The Bridegroom was in the R.A.F. and the bestman was also in the R.A.F. uniform. The bestman rose to propose the Toast to the Bride and Groom, but you can imagine the reaction when he made a slip of the tongue and said ... "BRIDE AND GLOOM!"

Another story relates to a situation where the bride's father was somewhat nervous about the speech he would have to make, and so he asked a rather inexperienced typist to type out what he would have to say. One of the guests was the headmistress of the school which the bride had attended as a little girl. Unfortunately the typist missed the letter "r" at a very important point in the speech and so it read...

"My daughter is very pleased that so many of you have come to share in the happiness of this day, and particulary she would want me to give a special welcome to someone from the school where she was educated, I refer, of course, to her Old FIEND the Headmistress."

REV DERMOT MCMORRAN BANGOR

MINISTER of TRINITY PRESBYTERIAN CHURCH

Perhaps the best story is that of a little girl who lived near the Newtownards Road in Belfast and each time there was a wedding in the Church on the Newtownards Road, she would stand outside to watch for the arrival of the Bride and then, when the Service was over, the departure of the guests. The Minister noticed that she seemed to be present at every wedding, so he spoke to her, and asked if she was interested in weddings. Her reply surprised him ...

"I'm very interested in the weddings in your Church, and when I get married, I want to get married here!"

The Minister asked if it was the beauty of the Church or the Order of Service which had a special appeal for her, but her reply was unexpected, and offered in the Ulster dialect ...

"It's not the Church, and it's not the Order of Service, but I've been watching the weddings here over a long time, and everyone of the Brides comes in with an oul' fella and goes out with a young wan!"

(She wasn't aware that it is the custom for the bride to be brought to the Church by the father and given away... and then to leave the Church with the Groom.)

REV.T.P.DONNELLY P.P.

St. Mary's Parochial House
Irish Green Street
LIMAVADY

HERE ARE A COUPLE OF QUOTATIONS YOU MIGHT USE:

Don't praise marriage on the third day, but after the third year. (Russian proverb)

All marriages are happy. It's the living together afterwards that causes all the trouble.

Marriage is like twirling a baton, turning handsprings or eating with chopsticks. It looks easy till you try it.

St. John's Parish Church, Coleraine

Rector: CANON H.H. WOODHEAD, B.A., H.Dip.Ed.
St. John's Rectory, Laurel Hill, Coleraine.
Phone: 2629

This is the true story of an event which took place many years ago in an Ulster farming community. An old farmer had 2 daughters - Mary and Martha and although Mary came in handy for the ploughing, Martha was the prettier of the two and unquestionably the best cook. One day a young man approached the farmer and requested Martha's hand in marriage. The farmer agreed and the date for the wedding was set. Weeks went by and there was no sign of the young man coming to court his fiancee. Eventually the farmer called on the young man to inquire whether the marriage was to proceed. "Aye surely", he was told "there'll be enough curtin' once we're wed.

The farmer went away and contemplated the situation. He came to the conclusion that the young man was not really too keen after all on Martha and certainly didn't deserve her. As he thought, he considered that it might be harder to find a husband for Mary so she would be the bride and Martha could be found another husband.

The wedding day dawned and the guests met at the church. Mary arrived as the bride, and the groom made no comment and the service proceeded as normal until the vow which included the phrase "from this day forward." "From this day fortnight", said the young man. The rector repeated the vow. "From this day fortnight", insisted the young man. Suspecting the influence of whiskey and being aware of the young man's educational record, the rector considered it a genuine mistake and continued with the service which concluded without further incident.

Two weeks later a knock came to the rectory door. "I'm here to have the weddin' disanulled", announced the young man on the doorstep. "She wasn't the one I'd bargained for and the fortnights up - I tried her but I don't like her."

Needless to say, the marriage wasn't disanulled and the couple had a long life together and raised a large family.

QUOTATIONS

It is a woman's business to get married as soon as possible and a man's to keep unmarried as long as he can.

George Bernard Shaw

Before marriage, a man will lie awake thinking about something you said; after marriage, he'll fall asleep before you finish saying it.

Helen Rowland

Marriage : a ceremony in which rings are put on the fingers of the lady and through the nose of the gentleman.

Herbert Spencer

Marriage is a mistake every man should make.

George Jessel

A woman worries about the future until she gets a husband, a man begins to worry about it when he gets a wife.

(unknown)

To get married is to tie a knot with the tongue that cannot undo with your teeth.

There is really no difference between an old maid and a married woman. The old maid is always lookings for a husband and so is the married woman.

Men are like fish, neither would get into trouble if they kept their mouths shut.

Love is like the measles - all the worse when it comes late in life.

Bigamy is having one wife too many. Monogamy is the same.

Keep they eyes wide open before marriage, and half shut afterward.

A good wife maketh a good husband.

A good husband should be deaf and a good wife blind.

(French Proverb)

Index

ACKNOWLEDGEMENTS

I would like to thank the following people, Graham Patterson for his brilliant and very clever illustrations. Bill Nesbitt, for two very funny and witty wedding poems. Robin Duke for his excellent art work and Mrs Edna Doherty for her always reliable typing skills.

Also Janet for proof-reading and the Girl Guide Leaders, Stephanie, Jane and the other members of the Guide Company for all their help and assistance.

Thank you to all the Clergy who contributec stories and jokes, and although unable to use them all they were very much appreciated.

Tommy Millar

Editor